EXPLORING
ANCIENT
CIVILIZATIONS

7

Marriage – Nero

Marshall Cavendish

N   dney

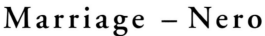

Marshall Cavendish
99 White Plains Road
Tarrytown, New York 10591-9001

www.marshallcavendish.com

Consultants: Daud Ali, School of Oriental and African
Studies, University of London; Michael Brett, School
of Oriental and African Studies, London; John
Chinnery, School of Oriental and African Studies,
London; Philip de Souza; Joann Fletcher; Anthony
Green; Peter Groff, Department of Philosophy,
Bucknell University; Mark Handley, History
Department, University College London; Anders
Karlsson, School of Oriental and African Studies,
London; Alan Leslie, Glasgow University Archaeology
Research Department; Michael E. Smith, Department
of Anthropology, University at Albany; Matthew
Spriggs, Head of School of Archaeology and
Anthropology, Australian National University

Contributing authors: Richard Balkwill, Richard
Burrows, Peter Chrisp, Richard Dargie, Steve Eddy,
Clive Gifford, Jen Green, Peter Hicks, Robert Hull,
Jonathan Ingoldby, Pat Levy, Steven Maddocks, John
Malam, Saviour Pirotta, Stewart Ross, Sean Sheehan,
Jane Shuter

WHITE-THOMSON PUBLISHING
Editors: Alex Woolf and Kelly Davis
Design: Derek Lee
Cartographer: Peter Bull Design
Picture Research: Glass Onion Pictures
Indexer: Fiona Barr

MARSHALL CAVENDISH
Editor: Thomas McCarthy
Editorial Director: Paul Bernabeo
Production Manager: Michael Esposito

Library of Congress Cataloging-in-Publication Data
Exploring ancient civilizations.
    p. cm.
Includes bibliographical references and indexes.
  ISBN 0-7614-7456-0 (set : alk. paper) -- ISBN 0-7614-7457-9 (v. 1 :
alk. paper) -- ISBN 0-7614-7458-7 (v. 2 : alk. paper) -- ISBN
0-7614-7459-5 (v. 3 : alk. paper) -- ISBN 0-7614-7460-9 (v. 4 : alk.
paper) -- ISBN 0-7614-7461-7 (v. 5 : alk. paper) -- ISBN 0-7614-7462-5
(v. 6 : alk. paper) -- ISBN 0-7614-7463-3 (v. 7 : alk. paper) -- ISBN
0-7614-7464-1 (v. 8 : alk. paper) -- ISBN 0-7614-7465-X (v. 9 : alk.
paper) -- ISBN 0-7614-7466-8 (v. 10 : alk. paper) -- ISBN 0-7614-7467-6
(v. 11 : alk. paper)
  1. Civilization, Ancient--Encyclopedias.
  CB311.E97 2004
  930'.03--dc21
                                    2003041224

ISBN 0-7614-7456-0 (set)
ISBN 0-7614-7463-3 (vol. 7)

Printed and bound in China

07 06 05 04 03 5 4 3 2 1

Contents

Marriage

Marriage, the formal union of a man and a woman, existed in some form in all ancient civilizations, although the range of wedding rituals, customs, and practices varied widely. For example, some societies permitted men to have more than one wife at the same time (polygamy), while others insisted that a man be married to only one wife (monogamy). Whatever form it took, marriage was one of the most important bonds holding ancient societies together.

▼ A miniature carving showing the Roman emperor Tiberius, his mother, Livia, and other members of their family. As Livia had been married to the previous emperor, scenes like these helped establish Tiberius's claim to the throne.

Marriage had social, legal, and political purposes. Socially it provided a man and a woman with comfort and security in their relationship. Although it was a public commitment, made by two people to one another, it seems unlikely that a man and a woman married because they loved each other. Love was generally seen as something that might develop between a couple after marriage rather than before.

Marriage and the Law

Marriage had many legal functions. First, it protected offspring. Children of a married couple were legitimate. A child had two adults who were responsible for his or her upbringing and welfare. Legitimate children were entitled to inherit their parents' property, social position, name, and title.

In many early societies a person's ancestry was vitally important; it explained who the person was. For example, the long family histories in the Old Testament of the Bible illustrate how important ancestry was to the Jewish people. Legitimate inheritance was also important to the thirty royal dynasties of ancient Egypt.

Marriage gave a couple legal protection. This protection was especially important for women. In many societies a husband could not just cast aside an aging wife because he wanted a younger one. In early China, as in all ancient civilizations, the law said that a man had a legal duty to look after his wife even if she no longer pleased him. Her family would usually make sure that justice was done.

Marriage and Politics

Political marriages were important only for the ruling classes. They were used to cement agreements and alliances between states or great families. For instance,

Tiberius, a future Roman emperor, was ordered to divorce his first wife and marry the daughter of Emperor Augustus. As Tiberius's mother had recently become the emperor's second wife, Tiberius became the emperor's stepson and thus was in a good position to become emperor himself—as he did when Augustus died in 14 CE.

Ceremonies and Rituals

Every society had its own form of marriage ceremony. However, some generalizations can be made about marriage customs in different parts of the ancient world.

In ancient Egypt there is surprisingly little evidence of any special ceremony associated with marriage. Marriage did not seem to involve religion. A man and woman simply set up house together. It appears that marriages in ancient Egypt were comparatively easily entered into and just as easily dissolved by either party, since Egyptian men and women had relatively equal rights. A marriage was usually dissolved if the couple was childless. Friends and neighbors seem to have made sure that the separating couple shared their possessions fairly.

MARRIAGE IN THE ROMAN EMPIRE INVOLVED MANY RULES:

In unions of the sexes, it should always be considered not only what is legal, but also what is decent.
If the daughter, granddaughter, or great-granddaughter of a senator should marry a freedman, or a man who practices the profession of an actor, or whose father or mother did so, the marriage will be void.

MODESTINUS, A ROMAN LAWYER, C. 250 CE

◀ This image of Egyptian marriage, dating from the fourteenth century BCE, shows Ankhesenpaaten attending to her husband Tutankhamen.

The ancient Egyptian king Tuthmosis I had a son, also named Tuthmosis, and a daughter, Hatshepsut. The royal brother and sister were officially married and had a daughter. In most societies such a union would have been condemned, but not in ancient Egypt. Marriage between close relatives was common in Egyptian royal families, although relatively few such marriages produced children, and kings were often born to secondary or minor wives. This freedom emphasized the status of the royal siblings. As gods and goddesses, they were not bound by the same laws as ordinary people.

In ancient Rome, a very legalistic society, marriage was much more complicated. There were, in fact, three types of marriage. One, known as *usus*, was informal, similar to marriage in ancient Egypt. *Coemptio* was more formal, while *confarreatio* was extremely complicated and expensive. Entered into by upper-class families, *confarreatio* involved a legal ceremony before many witnesses, processions, animal sacrifices to please the gods, and feasting. Roman marriage put a wife completely under her husband's control, almost as if she were a child.

In early India the long wedding ceremony centered around the couple's domestic hearth. A marriage was a permanent bond. Some groups took this idea to an extreme: when a husband died before his wife, she was expected to lie beside his body on the funeral pyre and be burned to death.

The giving of rings was common to many wedding ceremonies, as was the giving of a dowry. A dowry was a valuable gift of money or possessions, given by the bride's family and brought by the bride to her husband. In the Pacific islands of Melanesia, where polygamy was allowed, a tribal chief could build up a great deal of power and wealth in the form of dowries from his many wives.

◄ This Greek red-figure vase of the mid-fifth century BCE shows a bride preparing for her wedding.

SEE ALSO
• China • Egypt • Matriarchy and Patriarchy
• Men • Roman Republic and Empire • Women

Masada

Masada is a rock fortress 1,500 feet (457 m) high, on the western shore of the Dead Sea. According to the historian Flavius Josephus, in 73 CE a garrison of 960 Jews committed mass suicide there rather than submit to their Roman besiegers.

The Jewish Revolt

In 66 CE a Jewish national uprising against Roman rule was sparked off by the brutality of the Roman procurator (governor), Gessius Florus. The rebels made a surprise attack on Masada, killed the small Roman garrison, and seized the large stores of weapons there. These weapons were taken to Jerusalem and used in a successful attack on the Roman troops.

However, the rebels had no hope of securing a final victory against the Roman Empire. In 70 Jerusalem was retaken and destroyed. The Jews had lost the war, but they held out in Masada for three more years.

Masada's rebel leader, Eleazer ben Yair, belonged to a determined rebel group, the *Sicarii* (daggermen), named after the short, curved daggers the members hid under their clothes. At Masada, Eleazer ben Yair was head of a Jewish community of 960, including men, women, and children.

Roman Siege

In the winter of 72 the Roman Tenth Legion, commanded by Flavius Silva, besieged Masada. Silva constructed a wall around the rock to prevent anyone from escaping and built eight camps for his 15,000 troops. The earth banks of these camps can still be seen.

The Romans knew they could not starve out the defenders, who were well supplied, so they built a huge earth ramp on the western side. Then they dragged a siege tower and battering ram to the top and began to pound down the walls.

◀ A painting of the besieged rock fortress of Masada, with the Roman camps below. The Romans built a three-mile (4,500 m) wall around Masada.

According to Josephus, during the night before the final assault, the defenders chose to die by their own hands. By drawing lots, ten men were picked to kill all the others; those picked killed the others by cutting their throat. Then lots were drawn again, and one man was chosen to kill the remaining nine, before stabbing himself with a sword.

When the Romans broke in the following morning, they were astounded to find rows of dead bodies. Only two women and five children, who had been hiding in a cistern, survived to tell what had happened.

The Myth of Masada

The story of Masada has such great symbolic importance for the modern state of Israel that Israeli schoolchildren visit the fortress and army units hold swearing-in ceremonies there.

Yet Josephus was thought by some to be an unreliable historian who wrote much of his book to justify his own treacherous behavior during the revolt—he switched his loyalty from the Jews to the Romans. Historians, in fact, have found inconsistencies in his version of the mass suicide; it is also contradicted by archaeological evidence. All that is known for certain is that the fortress at Masada was captured in 73, finally ending the first Jewish revolt.

FOLLOWING IS AN EXCERPT OF THE SPEECH IN WHICH ELEAZER RECOMMENDS SUICIDE TO HIS COMPANIONS:

Let us die unenslaved by our enemies, and leave this world as free men in the company of our wives and children. This is what the Law ordains, and that is what our wives and children demand of us.

FLAVIUS JOSEPHUS, *THE JEWISH WAR*

▶ *A view from the ruins on top of Masada. The outline of the Roman camp can be seen as a dark line on the far right of the picture.*

Masks

Masks have been used for a variety of reasons throughout history. As early as the Stone Age, animal masks, made from hide and bone, were worn during hunting rituals. The masks might have represented gods, who could bring a tribe good fortune in its hunting, or they might simply have let hunters get closer to their prey. In ancient Greece and Rome masks were associated with acting, and in Africa with birth, death, and fertility rituals.

In ancient times, as people started to live in settled communities and grow crops, they began to use masks in fertility ceremonies. During these rituals priests often wore masks to represent gods or spirits.

Theatrical Masks

Ancient Egyptian priests and priestesses wore masks to play the roles of deities during rituals at least as early as 1800 BCE. Three masks survive; two portray the jackal-headed god Anubis, and the third is of the household god Bes.

One of the most famous ancient Greek fertility rites was a festival dedicated to Dionysus, the god of nature. Long, poetic rituals were enacted during this festival, with priests and actors in masks representing gods and men.

The poet Thespis, who lived in the sixth century BCE, made the leading actors in his ritual plays wear white linen veils over their faces. In this guise they had the authority to speak as unseen gods. As Greek ritual gave way to theatrical drama, the masks were used to represent not only gods and worshipers but many different characters, including heroes and villains.

▼ *A marble copy of a mask worn by a comic actor playing a leading role, as either an old man or a slave. It was made some time in the first century BCE.*

AFRICAN MASKS

Africans started using masks for their rituals in prehistoric times. Made of wood and decorated with grasses, the masks had either human or animal faces.

African masks were used in ceremonies celebrating fertility, births, deaths, and important tribal gatherings. They were also worn during the meetings of secret societies. The wearers, who were always men, kept their masks locked away so that women would not touch them.

Over time the making of the actors' masks became an art in itself. Most were made of leather or painted canvas, molded on marble heads. They often fitted over the actor's head like a helmet, and they usually had a metal mouthpiece, which helped the actor project his voice to the back of the theater. The masks represented not only different characters but also different emotions, ages, and degrees of wealth.

The Romans copied the Greeks' use of masks but seem to have preferred comedies to tragedies. Roman actors, always men, wore a range of masks in order to appear as gods, demigods, heroes, and heroines.

Death Masks

From around 2180 BCE the ancient Egyptians started placing masks on the faces of the dead before they buried them. Made of cloth and covered in plaster, these masks were intended to allow the soul of the deceased to recognize and return to its physical body. Pharaohs and rich nobles had masks made of beaten gold and silver.

The ancient Romans made death masks out of wax, molded on the dead person's face. After the funeral the mask was kept by the family as a memento of the dead person.

◄ A mask made by the Bakuba tribe in the Congo. The striking pattern and intricate detail are typical of a people famed for weaving in raffia, a skill passed down from ancient times.

SEE ALSO

- Art • Bantu Culture • Drama • Egypt
- Festivals • Greece, Classical
- Mycenaean Civilization • Prehistory
- Sacrifices

Matriarchy and Patriarchy

*M*atriarchy means "rule by women." The word comes from the Latin *mater*, meaning "mother." It describes a society in which women have governing authority in their families and in politics. Patriarchy means "rule by men" and comes from the Latin word *pater*, meaning "father." A patriarchy is a society where men have greater authority.

Theories of Matriarchy

Several nineteenth-century archaeologists, including the Swiss Johann Bachofen, believed that early human communities were matriarchal. Bachofen argued that women in the first human groups had special skills in food gathering, food preparation, and childbearing. These skills were necessary for the community to survive and thus must have made women the most powerful people in their tribes.

Bachofen also thought that some early societies were matrilineal, that is, people traced their descent through their mother rather than their father, and land and property were handed down through daughters rather than sons. Bachofen believed that women must also have ruled these matrilineal societies. His findings were influenced by myths of powerful women, such as the Greek legend of the female Amazon warriors.

Bachofen's ideas were supported by the American anthropologist Lewis Henry Morgan, who studied Native American peoples, such as the Crow and the Iroquois. Morgan believed that women had much more power in these cultures than they do in the modern world.

In the early twentieth century archaeologists discovered many Neolithic clay and stone female figurines. Some argue that these figurines are evidence of a fertile mother goddess worshiped by early people who lived in matriarchies.

▼ This stone figure was made in what is now Romania sometime around 4000 BCE. The woman may be an ancient fertility goddess. Historians believe that Neolithic farmers worshiped such figures in the hope that their lands and animals would be more fertile.

THE AMAZONS

The Greeks had myths about the Amazons, a race of hardy female warriors. The geographer Strabo (c. 64 BCE–c. 23 CE) thought they lived in Asia, far beyond the Caspian Sea. Theirs was supposedly a society in which women held all the power. They were said to keep and raise their female children but kill or disable their sons at birth. The few male children who survived were kept as household servants.

The Amazons were thought to be tough warriors who enjoyed battle as much as men. They were supposed to have cut off their right breast so that they could draw a bow or throw a spear more easily. Expert hunters and horse riders, they worshiped Ares (Mars), the god of war, and Artemis (Diana), the goddess of hunting.

The legendary Greek heroes Herakles (Hercules) and Theseus were both said to have traveled to the distant Amazon kingdom to compete and fight with Amazon queens. According to myth, the Amazons were finally defeated by the god Dionysus, who conquered them at Ephesus. Amazons were a popular subject in Greek and Roman art, often shown wearing short tunics or long trousers like those worn by Scythian horsemen.

Ancient Patriarchies

Modern archaeologists have found little evidence of ancient matriarchies. Female skeletons dating to Paleolithic and Neolithic times suggest that early women had much shorter lives than men; owing to the risks of repeated pregnancies, many women died quite young. Men tended to live longer and were able to gather more life experience, tribal knowledge, and authority. As in modern nomadic societies, early women probably stayed close to home, tending the fires and the children.

Most ancient societies were patriarchal. Roman and Hebrew fathers had the literal power of life and death over their families. Women in respectable Greek and Roman families seldom left their homes, except for weddings and funerals. In ancient China girls were considered inferior to boys, and women could not inherit property. In most ancient societies women took little part in public life.

▶ Amazons became a popular subject in Greek art around the end of the seventh century BCE. This fourth-century-BCE plate shows lightly armored Amazons in battle with Greek warriors.

Even in the most patriarchal societies, however, women still had influence. At the imperial Roman court the wives and mothers of emperors held enormous power. For example, the empress Agrippina, who lived from 15 to 59 CE, effectively ruled the Roman Empire for several years. She was even rumored to have poisoned her husband Claudius in order to help her son Nero replace him as emperor.

FEMALE PRESTIGE

Women were prominent figures in some ancient cultures, such as Celtic Ireland and Britain. Celtic noblewomen owned land and were often buried with symbols of wealth. There were at least two powerful Celtic British queens. Cartimandua ruled the warlike tribe of Brigantes, who lived along the northern borders of Roman Britain. Boudicca led her Iceni tribesmen in rebellion against Rome in 60 and 61 CE. Among the Pictish peoples of Caledonia (Scotland), names and land are thought to have been passed down through the mother's line.

Much earlier, one of Egypt's female pharaohs, Hatshepsut, born in about 1473 BCE, had been a very successful ruler of Egypt. Even the women of patriarchal Athens had their own areas of power. For instance, each autumn the women organized the three-day festival of Thesmophoria. This festival included secret rites to Demeter, the goddess of fertility, from which men were strictly excluded.

▶ Ancient Hebrew society was patriarchal. The duties and rights of Jewish women were strictly spelled out regarding religious family festivals, such as the Passover meal, depicted in this fourteenth-century-CE illustration.

SEE ALSO
- Agrippina • Boudicca • Celts • Families
- Hatshepsut • Marriage • Men • Women

Mauryan Empire

The Mauryans (c. 321–c. 200 BCE) were a family of kings who founded India's earliest empire. Under their rule India was politically united for the first time in history. At its height, in the third century BCE, the Mauryan Empire included all but the southern tip of India, modern Pakistan, and the eastern half of Afghanistan.

Chandragupta Maurya

Chandragupta Maurya was born in Magadha in about 340 BCE. Magadha, the most powerful of the northern Indian kingdoms, was ruled from the city of Pataliputra (modern Patna) by a dynasty called the Nandas.

According to tradition, Chandragupta formed a plot with one of the Nandas' ministers, whose name was Chanakya (or

Kautilya). Chanakya is credited with writing a well-known book on practical politics called the *Arthashastra* (Treatise on Rule), though some historians believe that this book dates from a later period. Chanakya had been badly treated by the Nanda king and nursed a grudge against him. With the help of Chanakya, Chandragupta raised an army and launched a rebellion. Around 321 BCE he seized the throne and rewarded Chanakya by making him his chief minister.

After conquering the Punjab, where Alexander the Great had left several Macedonian garrisons, Chandragupta went on to take over the whole of northern India.

War with Seleucus

Between 305 and 304 BCE Chandragupta had to defend his empire against a second Macedonian invasion. It was led by Seleucus Nicator (the Conqueror), the general who had made himself ruler of the eastern half of Alexander's empire.

Chandragupta, at the head of an army that included three thousand war elephants, fought a great battle against Seleucus. The outcome is not known, though the two kings made a peace treaty and a marriage alliance. Seleucus gave Chandragupta his eastern Asian territories in return for five hundred elephants. These animals later brought Seleucus a great victory over his Macedonian rivals at the battle of Ipsus in 301 BCE.

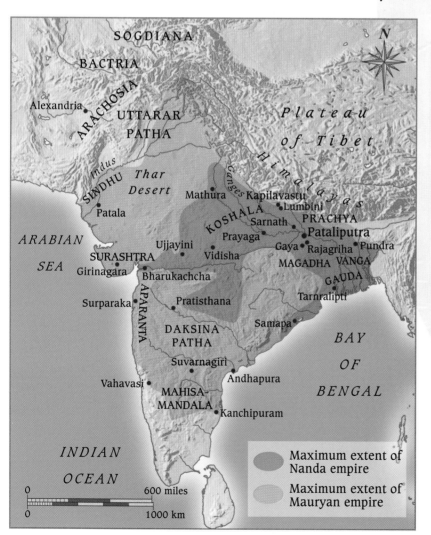

▼ The Nanda and Mauryan Empires at their fullest extents, between 365 and 185 BCE.

MAURYAN EMPIRE

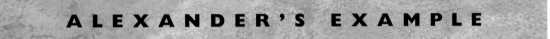

327 BCE

Alexander the Great invades India.

326 BCE

Alexander is forced to turn back after his army mutinies.

c. 321 BCE

Chandragupta Maurya overthrows the last Nanda king of Magadha.

305–304 BCE

Chandragupta fights a war with Seleucus Nicator, the Macedonian general who became king of much of Alexander's Asian empire.

c. 296–c. 270 BCE

Reign of Bindusara.

c. 268–239 BCE

Reign of Ashoka.

239–185 BCE

Mauryan Empire breaks up.

c. 185 BCE

Murder of Brhadratha, the last Mauryan king.

ALEXANDER'S EXAMPLE

It is no coincidence that the Mauryan Empire arose shortly after the invasion of India by the Macedonian king Alexander the Great. Alexander, who had conquered lands from Egypt to Afghanistan, brought the very idea of empire to India. Previously the country had been divided among many warring kingdoms.

Chandragupta Maurya, founder of the empire, was still a teenager in 327 BCE, when the Macedonians invaded. He met Alexander and watched him win an unbroken series of victories. Alexander's campaign ended only when his homesick soldiers mutinied in 326 and demanded to be led home.

According to the Greek biographer Plutarch, "in later years [Chandragupta] often remarked that Alexander was within a step of conquering the whole country." Alexander's example filled Chandragupta with ambition.

▼ Only a few stones remain of the Mauryan palace at Pataliputra, which is now covered by water.

Death by Starvation

Chandragupta eventually gave up his throne in favor of his son, Bindusara. Followers of the Jain religion preserve a tradition that Chandragupta had converted to their faith, which preached nonviolence to all living things. According to the Jains, this once great warrior king died in the manner of a Jain monk. He slowly starved himself to death in about 296 BCE.

Ruling the Empire

Seleucus sent an ambassador, Megasthenes, to the Mauryan court at Pataliputra in about 300 BCE. Megasthenes wrote a book, *Indica*, in which he described Indian customs, the Mauryan government, and the luxurious life of Chandragupta's court. Unfortunately the book is now lost, surviving only in fragments quoted by later writers.

According to Megasthenes, Mauryan rule was centralized and efficient. The government, in Pataliputra, oversaw all aspects of the economy. There was a well-organized civil service, with regional officers and local officials responsible for collecting taxes and checking weights and measures. Inspectors traveled the country using roads built and maintained by the government. They made sure that the local officials were doing their jobs properly and reported directly to the emperor.

Chandragupta encouraged agriculture by building irrigation canals and clearing land for farming. He used the taxes he raised from the farmers to pay for his vast standing army.

Later Rulers

Little is known of the second Mauryan emperor, Bindusara. He seems to have been another warrior king, for the Greeks knew him as Amitrochates, a name that comes from an Indian title meaning "slayer of enemies." During the twenty-six years of Bindusara's reign, Mauryan rule was extended into southern India.

▶ *A Mauryan terra-cotta figure of a woman wearing an elaborate headdress. This figure is similar to figures made by the earlier Indus valley peoples and is thought to be a goddess.*

The third and most famous Mauryan emperor was Bindusara's son, Ashoka, who became king in about 268 BCE. He had a very different personality from his father's and grandfather's. After fighting one war, Ashoka became horrified by the suffering he had caused and turned his back on violence. He converted to Buddhism and founded monasteries and built sacred stupas (mound-shaped monuments). All over his empire he had inscriptions carved explaining his new devotion to peace. In his Sixth Major Rock Edict, he wrote, "There is no better work than promoting the welfare of the whole world. Whatever may be my great deeds, I have done them in order to discharge my debt to all beings."

After Ashoka's death in 239 BCE, if not before, the Mauryan Empire began to break up. The reasons are not known. Perhaps Ashoka was unable to hold such a large territory together without the threat of warfare.

Historians know of six more Mauryan kings who ruled after Ashoka. Their territory gradually shrank until all that remained was the kingdom of Magadha, first seized by Chandragupta. In about 185 BCE Brhadratha, the last Mauryan king of Magadha, was murdered by Pushyamitra Shunga, the commander in chief of his army. The Mauryans were replaced by a new dynasty, the Shungas, and India was once again divided into warring kingdoms.

SEE ALSO
• Alexander the Great
• Ashoka
• Buddhism
• Hinduism
• Macedonians
• Pataliputra
• Sanchi

◀ *Emperor Ashoka's Great Stupa, at Sanchi in central India, was enlarged and decorated by later rulers. These carvings on the north gate date from the first century BCE.*

Maya

The civilizations, culture, and languages of the Maya people emerged in Central America around 1000 BCE. The area occupied by the Maya was shaped like a large triangle, covering the eastern part of present-day Mexico and the western parts of Guatemala, Belize, and Honduras. The Maya lived in communities, whether in remote villages or big cities. They were skilled jewelers and craftspeople and had great understanding of astronomy and mathematics. The Mayan cities were trading centers as well as places where religious rituals were held. Built as they were in the midst of thick forests, Tikal, Palenque, and the other great Mayan cities became largely inaccessible when the Mayan civilization declined; some cities lay undiscovered for hundreds of years.

▼ *The civilization and city-states of the Maya during their classic period (250–800 CE).*

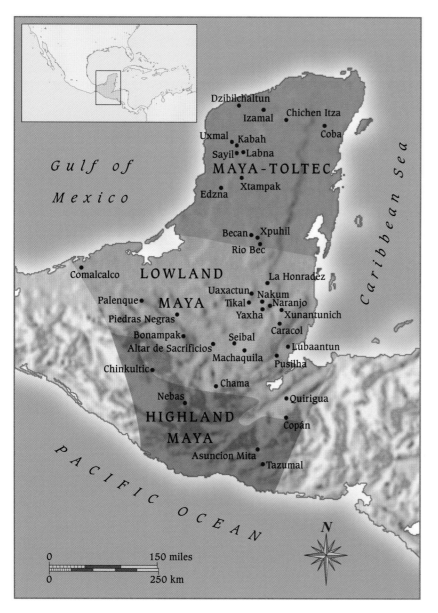

In Mayan communities families worked together to grow crops, to hunt, and to fish. Water was often hard to find so the Maya used sinkholes in the ground called cenotes. Water would flow naturally into them from the limestone rock; the ponds and lakes formed were used for bathing and drinking.

Then as now, climatic conditions varied dramatically over the vast extent of the Mayan landscape. The south had snow-capped mountains and towering volcanoes. Much of the rest of the territory was densely forested; there the climate was hot and damp with abundant rainfall.

In the great Mayan cities pyramids served as platforms for temples; some contained tombs. Stelae (inscribed stone slabs or pillars) were carved to commemorate great ancestors or victories in war.

At the heart of Tikal was the central acropolis, a palace. Here the *ahau*, both ruler and high priest, made decisions about justice, war, and ritual sacrifice.

Food and Farming

To the Maya people, corn was the most important crop. It was even considered to be a great god. Workers cleared parts of forests

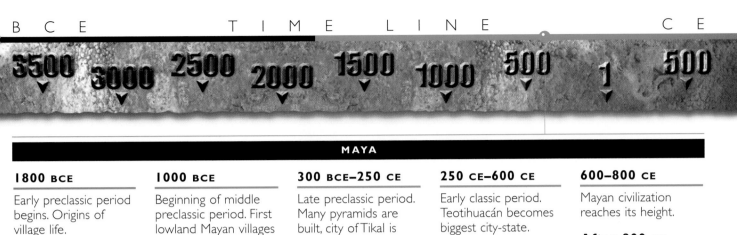

3500 **3000** **2500** **2000** **1500** **1000** **500** **1** **500**

MAYA

1800 BCE

Early preclassic period begins. Origins of village life.

1000 BCE

Beginning of middle preclassic period. First lowland Mayan villages appear.

300 BCE–250 CE

Late preclassic period. Many pyramids are built, city of Tikal is founded.

250 CE–600 CE

Early classic period. Teotihuacán becomes biggest city-state.

600–800 CE

Mayan civilization reaches its height.

After 800 CE

Classic Mayan civilization declines.

▼ *The ceremonial site of the Mayan city of Palenque, located in present-day Chiapas, Mexico. The Temple of the Inscriptions is on the left.*

by burning the trees and forming fields called milpa. The ash from the fires made the ground fertile for growing corn and beans. Farmers ground the ears of corn into flour to make flat bread, such as tortillas, or to make a drink called *balche*. Sometimes the flour was mixed with chilies and beans.

When the hunting and fishing were good, the Maya people ate anything they caught, including deer, monkeys, and even dogs, as well as turtles and frogs. Avocado pears and breadfruit grew in the forests.

IN THE 1840S JOHN LLOYD STEPHENS AND FREDERICK CATHERWOOD EXPLORED THE CENTRAL AMERICAN JUNGLE IN THE PRESENT-DAY PROVINCE OF YUCATÁN. THEY DISCOVERED THE CITIES OF PALENQUE, UXMAL, AND CHICHEN ITZA. IN 1843 STEPHENS WROTE ABOUT THE MAYA AND THE INDIANS WHO LIVED THERE THEN:

These cities ... are not the works of people who have passed away ... but of the same great race which ... still clings around their ruins.

JOHN LLOYD STEPHENS, *INCIDENTS OF TRAVEL IN CENTRAL AMERICA, CHIAPAS AND THE YUCATÁN*

Jade burial mask found in the Temple of the Inscriptions at Palenque.

The Maya made jewelry from jade, a fine blue-green stone thought to be a gift from heaven. They also used obsidian, a natural glass formed from cooling lava, to make knife blades. They made pots and vases from clay, which were fired and then decorated with bright colors. Seashells and precious stones were used to make ornaments for men and women; they were worn as bracelets around the wrist or as ankle bands.

Language and Writing

The Maya people had their own written language, formed of picture symbols known as glyphs. By studying the glyphs on carvings, stelae, tombs, and books made from beaten bark paper, experts can trace a detailed history of Mayan civilization. However, the rulers who ordered the histories to be carved apparently liked to justify their own actions, so the written record may not always give a true version of events. Historians therefore are required to act like detectives, piecing together the facts.

In the city of Quirigua, a series of beautiful stelae records the shapes of animal gods. The largest is over thirty-six feet (12 m) in height. At the top there is a glyph that represents the date when the Maya believed time began: 3113 BCE.

The Maya used honey as a sweetener, and dedicated a whole month of their calendar to the god of the bees. Cocoa pods were another crop, but they were not used to make chocolate. Instead they were mixed with water and pepper to make a very strong drink.

Arts and Crafts

Maya men and women made many kinds of decorative clothes and crafts. Apart from simple loincloths and colored mantas (square cloaks or shawls), people dressed in robes made of fine colored material and decorated with feathers from showy birds, such as the macaw. The quetzal, a rare bird captured for its beautiful tail feathers, was considered sacred and always released.

The Maya as Scientists

For the Maya people, science and religion were inseparable. They worshiped the gods that they believed controlled their destiny, while also studying weather patterns and astronomy. For example, they believed that the movements of the sun, moon, and stars directed their fortune in life. To the Maya, the full moon was a symbol of the mother of gods, cradling a rabbit in her arms.

MAYAN CALENDARS

The Maya had many calendars, including a sacred one called the tzolkin and one for farming known as the haab. The tzolkin had a 260-day cycle based on a counting system that used the unit 20. This unit may have been chosen because 20 is the number of fingers and toes on a human body. The 260 days were broken down into 13 numbers and 20 day names.

In the haab (the farming calendar) the Maya did not use the phases of the moon to create a 12-month year. Instead they broke the 365 days into 18 "months" of 20 days each, with a short 5-day month to make up the total. Joined together, the two timescales formed a cycle of 18,980 days, or 52 years.

▼ This fragment shows calculations made by the Maya as they observed the stars, moon, planets, and sun. The Maya used these calculations to make their calendars.

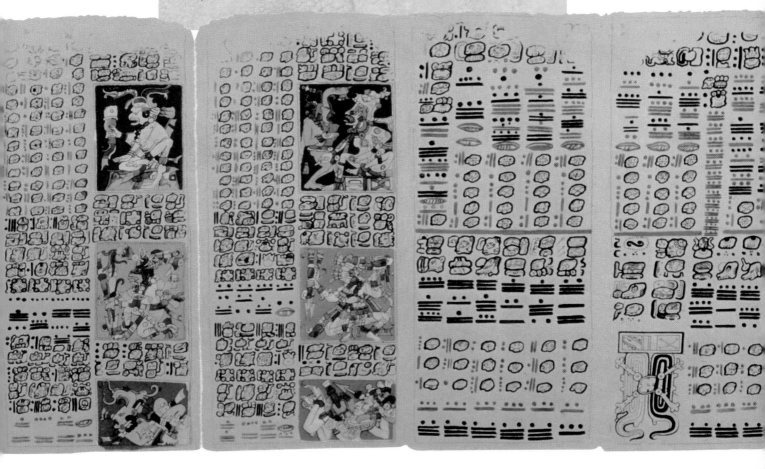

MAYAN MATHEMATICS

The Maya people invented the concept of zero. In their system of numbering, a dot represented 1, a bar was 5, and a shell symbol was 0. They used numbers for trading and to construct their elaborate calendars. By studying the movements of the moon and the planet Venus, they came very close to correctly estimating the length of the lunar month (29.53 days) and the year of Venus (584 days).

This terra-cotta carving of a priest in front of a funnel served as an incense burner. The priest, who may represent the sun god, is standing on a turtle from which the god of the underworld emerges.

Ritual and War

The royal scepter in the court of Tikal shows the emblem of Bolon Tzaicat, half man, half god, who protected the generations of ruling families. Creatures like the quetzal and the jaguar were also symbols of beauty, strength, and power.

Historians believe some Mayan cities were destroyed because their rival rulers fought constantly. To many *ahau*, the spiritual and political rulers of the cities, war was necessary to capture prisoners to sacrifice to their fierce gods. Buluk Chaptan was the god of violent death; his outstretched hand looks as if it is seizing a victim.

Wars usually took place in the dry season, because farmers could then leave their land and fight. Warriors dressed up in magnificent headdresses and painted themselves in red and black, the colors of blood and death. They used lances with flint points or *macanas* (swords with wooden hilts and obsidian blades).

SEE ALSO
- Calendars • Sacrifices • Tikal • Writing

Melanesian Culture

Many tens of thousands of years ago, dark-skinned peoples from Southeast Asia started to settle in the Pacific area now known as Melanesia. West of Polynesia and south of Micronesia, Melanesia as a region is often divided up into two parts: New Guinea, the largest land mass in the region, and various islands and island groups, including the Bismarck Archipelago, Fiji, the Solomon Islands, Vanuatu, and New Caledonia. Until the end of the Ice Age, New Guinea was joined to Australia to form a much larger landmass, and thus the earliest peoples of both places are probably related.

Many Lands, Many Languages

Although often considered one region, a large range of different ancient groups and cultures developed on the Melanesian islands, sometimes influenced by other civilizations, including the Polynesians. The Melanesians had no written language, but researchers estimate that about nine hundred different languages were spoken. The many different groups were often in conflict with each other.

Farmers and Gatherers

In some parts of New Guinea, there were large settlements of over a thousand people. In most of ancient Melanesia, however, people tended to live in much smaller groups of under a hundred. The Melanesians lived off both the sea and the land. To prepare ground for planting crops, they cleared areas of rain forest with stone tools and sometimes used fire as well. Digging sticks and paddle-shaped wooden spades were used to break up the soil, and crops such as taro, yams, and plantains (a relation of the banana) were planted. The pig was the main farm animal in much of Melanesia, while fishing, hunting, and gathering wild foods, such as nuts and fruit, were also important sources of food.

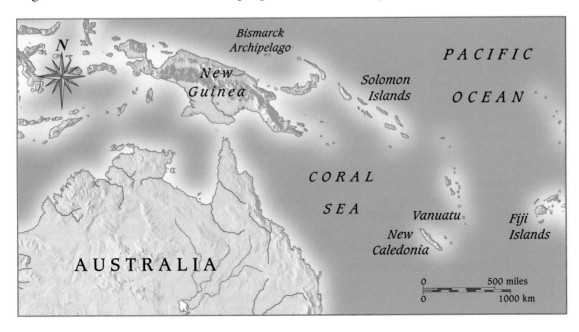

The geographical area of Melanesia.

MELANESIAN CULTURE

40,000–30,000 BCE

First peoples reach Melanesia and settle in New Guinea, the Bismarck Archipelago, and the Solomon Islands.

c. 7000 BCE

Papuan peoples start farming root vegetables.

1300–900 BCE

Lapita people settle in parts of Melanesia. Vanuatu, New Caledonia, and Fiji are settled for the first time.

1568 CE

Spanish explorer Don Alvaro de Mendaña y Neyra discovers Solomon Islands.

1643 CE

Abel Tasman is the first European to reach Fiji.

▶ This elaborate crested mask, which represents the soul of a dead person, originates from New Ireland, part of Papua New Guinea. It is made from wood and shells and would be worn as a helmet.

MELANESIAN ARTS AND CRAFTS

Ancient Melanesians did not have metals, and only some of these early peoples worked clay into pottery. They all wove cloth and made bags, fishing nets, and ropes out of plant fibers and tree bark. They used stone and shell tools to carve wood and stone. Giant bamboo was carved to produce water containers, cooking vessels, and torches, and the wood from local trees was carved into shields and masks.

In some parts of ancient Melanesia, masks were far more than an art form. They were used in important ceremonies and often worn to represent a mythical being or the spirit of an ancestor. In many parts of New Guinea, the people used their artistry on their own bodies, decorating themselves with complicated face and body painting and large, colorful headdresses.

Trading Resources

On larger islands, such as Fiji, the people were often split into coastal dwellers, who largely lived off the sea, and inland groups, who relied on farming and gathering. On many islands inland groups would regularly trade food they had grown and gathered for fish, for salt, which was prized as a way of adding taste to food, and for shells, which were needed to make jewelry.

▲ *Kava drinking ceremonies, like this one in Fiji, were popular throughout Melanesia.*

Archaeologists have discovered that trade also occurred between islands, owing to the different resources that were available in different areas. For example, there was a demand for obsidian—a volcanic glass that could be worked to make tool blades. Obsidian did not exist on all islands. Likewise, there was a need for pigs, clay to make pottery, certain types of beads made from shells, and suitable wood for canoes. The Melanesians traveled using dugout canoes made from hollowed-out tree trunks, similar to those of the ancient Micronesians and Polynesians.

Melanesian Beliefs

Although religious beliefs varied in different parts of Melanesia, they usually combined ancient stories and myths, rituals, magic, and worshiping of ancestors. In many parts of Melanesia, the ancient peoples believed that their ancestors' spirits were still present and watched over them to make sure that society's rules were obeyed

KAVA CEREMONIES

Kava is a type of drink made from the root of a plant related to the pepper tree. It relaxes the body and increases sensitivity to sight and sounds. In parts of ancient Melanesia kava was the traditional drink of chiefs and was used in many ceremonies and rituals. On some islands women were banished from such ceremonies on pain of death; on others women were allowed to attend.

and its rituals were carried out. Witchcraft was sometimes practiced; spells were used for success in farming, in battle, and in marriage. The notion that people and objects had spiritual power, known as mana, was a common belief in Polynesia and was also widespread in Melanesia.

SEE ALSO
- Lapita Culture
- Micronesian Culture
- Polynesian Culture
- Transportation

Men

Men held a position of dominance in virtually all ancient civilizations. Most societies had a male ruler, whether an emperor, a king, or a chief. No empress ever ruled the Roman Empire, for example, although at least six female pharaohs ruled in ancient Egypt. Men usually filled the more important religious positions, too; they were also the ministers, scribes, civil servants, judges, lawyers, generals, and soldiers.

Primitive Power?

Historians and anthropologists used to assume that males had dominated society since prehistoric times. This reasoning was based on men's physical characteristics. Men were stronger than women, more aggressive, and not limited by the need to breast-feed infants. In a primitive society, therefore, where hunting and fighting were vitally important, males dominated. This situation, it was argued, carried through into the early civilizations.

Since the middle of the twentieth century, however, experts have challenged this idea. Study of societies that have remained relatively unchanged over long periods of time, such as the Inuit of North America and the aborigines of Australia, suggests that in prehistoric times the relationship between men and women was quite equal. Indeed, the first all-powerful divinity was more likely to have been female than male: the great earth goddess was the bringer of all life.

Male Dominance

Male dominance may have emerged about 4,500 years ago. The key, it is argued, was that men realized that women could produce babies only with the participation of men. Therefore, men, not women, controlled the reproduction of the species. This understanding gave men confidence to match their physical strength and had a huge effect on all ancient civilizations.

This newly acquired confidence coincided with many other developments. In Mesopotamia and Egypt, for example, bronze tools and weapons appeared and tended to put more power into the hands of men. So too did the emergence of organized armies. Men joined the armies as soldiers, and male officers commanded them.

▼ *This second-century-CE marble relief depicts the all-male Roman Praetorian Guard. In many ancient societies, power simply meant physical strength.*

Writing was also essential to the development of male power. Once laws and customs placing men above women were written down, they tended to become permanent. In religion male gods, such as the Greek Zeus and the Jewish Jehovah, replaced earlier earth goddesses as the supreme power. Males controlled most of the priestly functions, too.

Coming of Age

No ancient civilization believed in a long period of male adolescence. The perceived change from boy to man happened quickly, often as the result of a ceremony or ritual. This rite of passage was the equivalent of the modern eighteenth or twenty-first birthday celebration, although it normally took place at an earlier age.

Circumcision featured in several coming-of-age rites, especially in Africa. In ancient Greece men became adults after a religious rite in which they had to swear allegiance to the god or goddess of their city. They were then free to marry, fight in the army, and in Athens, vote for political representatives.

GENDER IN ART

The art of ancient civilizations reflects their attitudes toward masculinity. The fact that the ancient Greeks frequently sculpted the male body indicates the great respect in which they held it. Even in ancient Egypt, where relations between men and women were more nearly equal than in almost any other early culture, the husband is at times shown larger than his wife in paintings and sculptures.

▶ This Greek sculpture of the third century CE, commonly entitled the Dying Gaul, celebrates the beauty of the male form.

Men and Women

In the male-dominated ancient world relationships between men and women were often like those between masters and servants. For instance, in Greece and Rome the position of women was inferior to that of the male members of the household. A married woman had to promise to serve and obey her husband. Unmarried women were under the control—and protection—of the male members of their family.

One of the most exclusively male societies was that of Sparta, the Greek city-state that rivaled Athens. Young Spartan men lived apart from women. They could not marry before the age of twenty, and even then, they were not permitted to live with their wives until the age of thirty.

Although men in the ancient world were generally perceived as being superior to women, all men were not in fact superior to all women. Slaves, for example, were inferior to all free people, male and female.

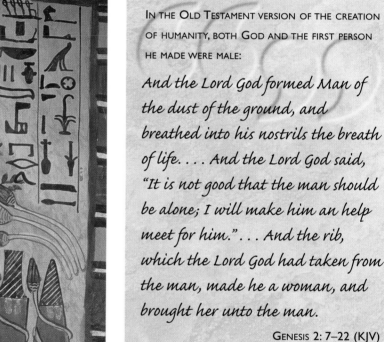

IN THE OLD TESTAMENT VERSION OF THE CREATION OF HUMANITY, BOTH GOD AND THE FIRST PERSON HE MADE WERE MALE:

And the Lord God formed Man of the dust of the ground, and breathed into his nostrils the breath of life. . . . And the Lord God said, "It is not good that the man should be alone; I will make him an help meet for him." . . . And the rib, which the Lord God had taken from the man, made he a woman, and brought her unto the man.

GENESIS 2: 7–22 (KJV)

▼ *An Egyptian wall painting from the second century BCE graphically shows the dominance of men over women: the huge figure of the nobleman Sennefer towers over his wife, Meryt.*

SEE ALSO
- Egypt • Greece, Classical • Marriage
- Matriarchy and Patriarchy • Women

Mesopotamia

Mesopotamia, a Greek word meaning "between the rivers," is the name of the fertile valley watered by the Euphrates and the Tigris Rivers, which flow through modern Syria and Iraq and into the Persian Gulf. The two rivers brought water and fertility to the dry land. Early inhabitants cultivated wheat and barley on the banks of the rivers. By building canals and dykes for irrigation, they produced more food than they needed just to survive. There, for the first time in history, cities were built. Wealth was built up by trading surplus food for other products not found locally. In this way some people were able to live without engaging in manual labor.

Mesopotamian civilization was characterized by the mixing of two peoples, the Sumerians, who lived in the far south, close to the gulf, and a different people living farther north, later known as the Akkadians. Powerful Akkadian kings, such as Sargon (around 2300 BCE), extended the influence of Mesopotamia by conquering neighboring territories. Powerful Mesopotamian kingdoms followed, such as the Babylonian Empire under Hammurabi and later Nebuchadrezzar II. The Assyrian Empire also arose in Mesopotamia, around 2000 BCE. The inhabitants of the various states did not have a single name for the area that became known as Mesopotamia.

▼ Mesopotamia under successive empires.

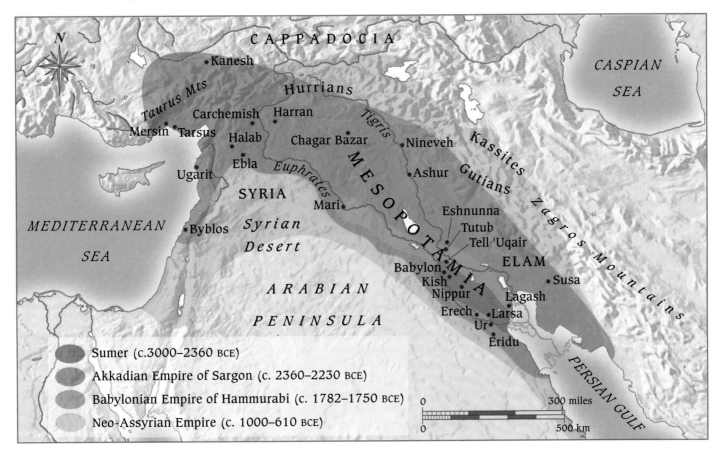

Sumer (c.3000–2360 BCE)

Akkadian Empire of Sargon (c. 2360–2230 BCE)

Babylonian Empire of Hammurabi (c. 1782–1750 BCE)

Neo-Assyrian Empire (c. 1000–610 BCE)

MESOPOTAMIA

c. 5000 BCE

Settlement is established at Erech.

c. 3000 BCE

Mesopotamian cities such as Erech, Eridu, and Ur become well established.

c. 2300 BCE

Akkadian state is established.

2000 BCE

Emergence of Assyrians.

1894 BCE

Emergence of Babylon.

c. 1350–c. 1000 BCE

Middle Assyrian Empire.

c. 1000–c. 610 BCE

Neo-Assyrian Empire.

562 BCE

Nebuchadrezzar II dies.

539 BCE

Mesopotamia is conquered by the Persians.

▼ *This helmet, made of electrum and covered with beaten gold, belonged to Mes-Kalam-Dug, king of Ur around 2500 BCE, and was found in the royal cemetery at Ur.*

Early Cities

The Sumerians built the first cities in Mesopotamia. Inhabitants of places such as Eridu, Ur, and Erech (modern-day Warka) used baked and unbaked bricks to make city walls and living quarters. Houses were built around a courtyard, often with no windows opening on to the street. The largest and highest building in these cities was a ziggurat, a temple tower consisting of stepped platforms inside a high wall. Its main purpose was to hold an elevated shrine, which had an important use in certain rituals.

The royal palace and the temples were usually situated on the main mound (*tell*, in Arabic). The priests lived in houses close by. The palace housed the king and his family and was also the center of government.

Also important in city life were the traders who exported surplus food to neighboring communities in exchange for building products such as wood and stone, as well as precious metals. Lapis lazuli, a deep-blue mineral used as a gemstone and imported from Afghanistan, was highly prized in Mesopotamia.

Traces of Everyday Life

In the nineteenth century scholars began searching in Iraq for places mentioned in the Bible. They found many Mesopotamian artifacts in the ruins of the ancient cities they discovered. In graves they found drinking bowls and other everyday objects, as well as helmets and finely crafted items of jewelry. Many beautiful objects were discovered, for example, bowls made from alabaster, a white material that can be finely ground down until the light shines through and polished with sand until it is smooth to the touch. Statues of priests, kings, and the gods have also been uncovered, along with remains of temple carvings.

Great Floods

Cities such as Ur and Eridu were built close to the water to take advantage of transport by river. However, their location also meant that they faced the threat of large floods. Conditions in this area may have inspired events in the *Gilgamesh Epic*, the earliest known epic poem. The compiler of the *Gilgamesh Epic* included an account of a great flood that resembles the one in the biblical story of Noah, though the Mesopotamian version was written much earlier, perhaps in the first half of the second millennium BCE.

The Mesopotamians were a highly practical people, as shown by their use of bitumen, a natural tar that can be used as a waterproofing coating. Some 350 miles (560 km) upstream from Ur, bitumen was found gushing up out of the ground. It was brought down the Euphrates to waterproof the city walls of Ur.

SCRIBES

Temple priests learned to read and write, and some of them became scribes. One clay tablet from Mesopotamia reads, "A scribe who does not know Sumerian, what [kind of] scribe is he?" Being the only ones who could read and write, scribes were valued by kings who wanted their own achievements to be recorded in royal inscriptions. Evidence suggests the scribes themselves recruited and trained students from within their own families or through a system of adoption. Scribes had to learn various skills because they might be asked to draw up architectural plans for buildings as well as write a variety of legal documents. One clay tablet records a boast by a scribe: "Sales of houses, of fields, of slaves male and female, silver guarantees, field rental contracts, contracts for planting palm-groves. . . . I know how to write all that."

▶ A Mesopotamian pottery bowl, dated around 3000 BCE, decorated with a geometric pattern.

This Mesopotamian tablet, from the late fourth millennium BCE, was first inscribed with pictographs and then baked and dried until almost as hard as stone.

Art and Writing

The achievements of Mesopotamian civilization were varied and impressive. For example, the people showed their intelligent inventiveness in the many ways in which they used clay. They built simple homes as well as grand ziggurats from mud bricks made from soft clay. Artistic and decorative figurines, along with jars and jar stoppers, were fashioned from clay. Their greatest achievement, the invention of writing, also depended on clay.

Tablets were shaped out of clay, and the soft material was pressed with a sharp tool, called a stylus, to form images, which were preserved by baking the clay. Many thousands of such tablets have been excavated. At first the image was a picture of the object represented. So, for example, corn was rep-resented by a picture of a sheaf of corn. Early writing recorded transactions such as wages and goods bought and sold. When it was realized that an image could stand for, not an object, but the sound of the word for an object, writing (in the modern sense) came into being. Writing developed in Mesopotamia earlier than in the civilizations of China and India.

Writing and art are combined in some of the beautiful cylinder seals that have been found by archaeologists. Although writing first developed in Mesopotamia, the vast majority of Mesopotamian people could not read or write, including most of the kings.

Although professional scribes had mastered the art of writing, important people still needed to be able to record their own

mark. A legal document, for instance, recording the purchase of a piece of land, required what is now called a signature. This requirement was met by the use of a seal made for a particular individual.

Cylinder seals were made of precious stone, such as alabaster, serpentine, or agate, or occasionally simply of baked clay. They were usually carved with pictures, and there was a hole in the middle to which a handle could be attached. The handle allowed the seal to be rolled across a damp clay tablet to create the "signature."

Mesopotamian culture also developed a counting system based, not on ten, as in the decimal system, but on sixty. The sexagesimal system, as it is called, is still used in units of time (for example, sixty minutes in an hour) and angle measurement (360 degrees in a circle).

THE MESOPOTAMIANS DEVELOPED THE WORLD'S FIRST WRITTEN LITERATURE. THIS EXTRACT IS FROM A POEM MOURNING THE DESTRUCTION OF A GREAT CITY, UR. THE POET LAMENTS:

That on the banks of the Tigris and Euphrates "bad weeds" grow,
That no one sets out for the road, that no one seeks out the highway,
That the city and its settled surroundings be razed to ruins,

. . . .

That the hoe not attack the fertile fields, that the seed not be planted in the
*   ground,*
That the sound of the song of the one tending the oxen not resound on the
*   plain,*

. . . .

That the song of churning not resound in the cattle pen.

CITED BY GWENDOLYN LEICK, MESOPOTAMIA

SEE ALSO
• Akkadians
• Babylon • Erech
• Eridu
• Gilgamesh Epic
• Nebuchadrezzar II
• Sargon of Akkad
• Sumer
• Ur
• Writing

Micronesian Culture

Micronesia is a region in the Pacific Ocean north of Melanesia. Micronesia means "small islands," and the region has over two thousand islands made of coral or volcanic rock. Micronesia occupies an area larger than that of the United States, but it is mostly ocean, with only 1,100 square miles (2,850 km^2) of land. Starting around 4,500 years ago, peoples from the Philippines, Indonesia, and Melanesia settled many of the Micronesian islands. They developed cultures that generally lasted intact until the arrival of European and American influence in the early 1800s.

Food and Drink

Those Micronesian people who lived on the higher, volcanic islands tended to have more fertile land than those living on lower-lying coral islands and atolls. Higher-island dwellers, such as the peoples on Yap, Palau, and the Marianas, grew taro, yams, breadfruit, and other crops. Rice was grown only on the Marianas, and some islanders kept animals such as dogs and pigs.

Fishing was a vital source of food, especially for those who lived on the lower islands, where there was less farmland. Both men and women fished. The women usually waded in the waters around the coral reefs. Only the men ventured out in canoes to fish in the deep sea.

Clans and Families

Micronesian societies were usually matrilineal, that is, the generations were traced through the mother. Families were grouped in clans, and the head clan on each island could trace its ancestors all the way back to the island's original settlers. Each extended family, with grandparents, cousins, and close relations, lived together in the same settlement. As the Micronesians had no written language, history was passed down orally through the generations.

Building Houses

Micronesian houses were built on raised platforms of rock and dirt using the local woods, such as mahogany. They were fitted with steeply sloping thatched roofs that reached down toward the ground to protect the dwellings against heavy tropical rains. The houses had little ventilation, and the smoke from a small fire helped keep mosquitoes away. In the Mariana Islands the houses of important people were raised high above the ground on stone pillars, called latte stones.

▼ The geographical area of Micronesia.

THE STONE-MONEY ISLAND

Ancient culture on Yap developed a little differently from that of other parts of Micronesia. Descent was traced through the father's and not the mother's line, and complicated dances, which told stories from the past, were performed. Yap was also unique in using carved limestone disks with a hole in the middle as money when the rest of ancient Micronesia was using beads, shells, and clams to conduct trade. This stone money, called rai, was quarried on the islands of Palau and Guam and transported by canoes and rafts to Yap. The size of the disks varied from 2 inches (5 cm) to 8 feet (2.4 m) in diameter. The largest examples, weighing several tons, can still be found lying alongside village paths around Yap.

MICRONESIAN CULTURE

c. 2500 BCE

Probable date of first settlement in the Mariana Islands, settled from the Philippines.

c. 2000–1500 BCE

Earliest dated remains of settlement on the Palau Islands, settled from Indonesia.

c. 100 BCE

The rest of Micronesia is settled by this date, probably from Melanesia.

600–800 CE

Start of islet building at Nan Madol on Pohnpei.

▶ *An example of the stone money found on Yap. Although not used as currency in other countries, stone money is still considered valuable on Yap.*

Micronesians had no metal to work with, and only some of the islanders worked clay to make pottery. All island groups, however, became skilled at working with stone and shell tools and produced wood and stone carvings, jewelry, and buildings.

Water Transport

Like other Pacific civilizations, such as the Melanesians and the Polynesians, the Micronesians relied on water transport.

The most common boat used by these peoples was the canoe, frequently made from the hollowed-out trunk of the breadfruit tree and fitted with a wooden float to one side called an outrigger.

The peoples on the high islands tended to travel only in the more sheltered waters around their islands. However, the peoples on low islands, such as the Marshalls and the Gilberts, ventured farther. They sometimes traveled for many days, carrying food both for themselves and as gifts in case they had to land on another island. These longer-distance voyagers built deeper, more stable ocean-going craft up to 100 feet (30 m) in length. They fitted cut planks to the sides of the canoes and sewed them together using strong cord made out of coconut fiber.

THE ISLETS OF NAN MADOL

Micronesian culture reached its height between 600 and 800 CE, when the inhabitants of the island of Pohnpei began building the ceremonial city of Nan Madol. The central part of the city was built on top of ninety-two man-made artificial islets, created by shifting over 500,000 tons of rock and coral. Archaeologists are still trying to solve the many mysteries surrounding Nan Madol and the remarkable feat of its construction.

▼ One of the side walls of Nan Douwas, the largest and most important islet of the Nan Madol complex. One of the corner stones at Nan Douwas weighs around 52 tons (47,000 kg).

SEE ALSO

Migration

Many ancient peoples migrated: they wandered from one home to another, taking their language, art, and religious beliefs with them. A whole people might move or only a relatively small part. For example, by 200 BCE the Polynesians were moving steadily eastward through the Pacific and reached Hawaii by about 800 CE. In the reign of the Indian king Ashoka (268–232 BCE), Buddhist priests traveled as missionaries west from India as far as Syria.

▼ This relief from Medinet Habu shows Ramses III about to smash his enemies' heads with a scimitar. His enemies—whom he is holding by the hair—are "peoples of the sea" and their Libyan allies.

Colonization

Colonization is a process whereby a people gains control of a foreign land by establishing a permanent settlement there. For several centuries the Greeks colonized the area around the Mediterranean. The philosopher Socrates said they were "like frogs round a pond." By 1500 BCE there were Greeks on the coast of Asia Minor, and from about 1200 BCE a new surge of migration took place there. Hemmed in by mountains, the Greeks often had little land that could be farmed and were forced to find more territory in which to grow crops.

There were other reasons to establish colonies. The Greeks may have moved west because of their fear of the Persians, and they probably moved to the islands of Corsica and Sicily in order to practice piracy as well as to trade. Taking over other people's lands often involved violence.

Upheaval and War

Throughout history, wars have created migrants and refugees. Around 1200 BCE in the Mediterranean, there were restless movements of violent, piratical, and perhaps displaced "peoples of the sea," as they were described by the Egyptians. In Egypt, during the reign of Ramses III (1184–1153 BCE), their attacks—in which they were supported by Libyan allies— appeared in temple scenes at Medinet Habu, although Ramses managed to stop them from invading Egypt.

Natural Disaster and Climate Change

Natural disasters, such as floods, droughts, and volcanic eruptions, caused several mass movements of ancient peoples. For example, the huge volcanic explosion on the Greek island of Thera, thought by some scholars to have occurred in 1625 BCE and by others in 1400 BCE, probably displaced thousands of people from nearby Aegean islands.

Migration or Invasion?

Peaceful migrations are sometimes seen as invasions. For instance, the Mycenaean kingdoms of Greece collapsed about 1200 BCE. A few hundred years later, in perhaps the tenth century BCE, the Dorians, a people speaking a dialect of Greek, drifted down from the western part of the Balkans into Greece. This migration may have been less a warlike invasion than a mass movement of displaced peoples.

Evidence for Migration

Various kinds of evidence suggest migratory movements. A story such as Homer's *Iliad* (describing the siege of Troy) or the Book of Exodus in the Old Testament (describing the Hebrews' journey from Egypt to Israel), may preserve folk memories of movement. Greek inscriptions mark the route the Dorians took through Greece as they came down from the northwest.

In Polynesia the distribution of the bones of domesticated animals that have been found shows that the people moved deliberately, taking precious belongings with them. Archaeologists have found evidence that suggests they traveled eastward from western Polynesia, taking with them plants of mainly Asian origin. In 1947 the Norwegian anthropologist Thor Heyerdahl sailed from South America in a craft such as the Polynesians might have used in order to prove that they had originally come from that continent. Others have argued that they came from British Columbia. Still others have claimed that the Polynesians colonized South America from Polynesia.

Sometimes the existence of similar customs in places far apart is taken to indicate contact. For instance, because both the Chinese and the Olmecs, who lived along Mexico's Gulf Coast, placed a piece of jade in the mouth of a dead person to ensure eternal life, some people believe the Olmecs had contact with the Chinese. This similarity could also simply be a coincidence.

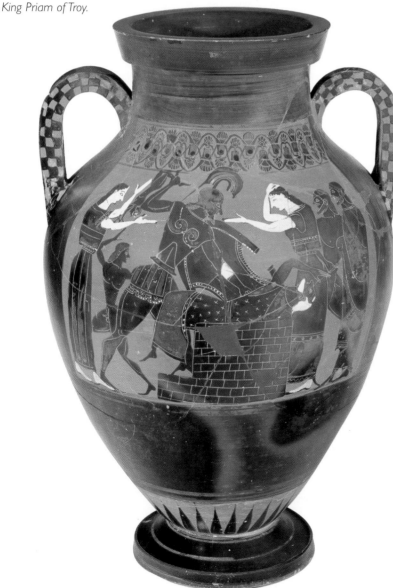

▼ *Greek stories of the Trojan wars, as recounted in Homer's* Iliad, *may have been told to preserve in memory a mass migration of Greek-speaking peoples to Asia Minor (modern-day Turkey), where Troy was located. In this scene, the Greek Neoptolemos kills King Priam of Troy.*

DID THE ARYANS INVADE INDIA AROUND 1500 BCE?

Horse-riding Aryans from Russia were once believed to have invaded India. They were said to have brought with them the Vedic religion, whose literature often mentions the horse, an animal the Indus valley peoples were not thought to have domesticated before 1500 BCE. The Aryans also worshiped gods of fire, drank warming drinks, and were warlike.

However, some scholars say there was no invasion. It is not mentioned in any Indian literature, they say. In addition archaeologists have shown that an Indus valley civilization existed continuously from about 4500 to 800 BCE, with lists of kings to 3000 BCE. They also point out that fire worshiping and horse breeding existed in the Indus valley long before the Aryans were thought to have introduced them. In fact, Vedic fire altars dating to the third millennium BCE have been found there, and the remains of a horse were discovered in Harappa, an ancient Indus valley settlement.

◄ In this scene from a Jewish prayer book of 1427 CE, Moses leads the Israelites across the Red Sea as they migrate to Canaan.

SEE ALSO
- Aryans • Athens • Indus Valley
- Lapita Culture • Melanesian Culture
- Minoans • Pottery • Ships and Boats

Minoans

Minoan civilization developed on the Greek island of Crete between about 3000 BCE and 1450 BCE, reaching its height after about 2000 BCE. Until the burning of many of the palaces in around 1450 BCE, Minoan Crete seems to have been prosperous and peaceful. Its people produced olive oil and wine, farmed, fished, made pottery, and worked gold. They also traded—with Egypt, western Asia, other islands in the Aegean Sea, mainland Greece, and to the west as far as Italy and maybe beyond.

Palaces seem to have been central to Crete's prosperity. Knossos was already a large settlement by about 3000 BCE. Other Cretan towns developed palaces similar to the one at Knossos, though not as large or complex. Phaistos, Gournia, and Khania had streets, public buildings, and many-roomed houses.

A great deal is known about the seemingly peaceful and artistic Minoans, but much remains a mystery. For example, there is no evidence of them ever going to war and none explaining how their palaces came to be burned down around 1450 BCE.

A Civilization without War?

Archeological evidence suggests that Cretan palaces lacked defensive walls. It appears that, for most of their history, the Minoans did not expect enemies on Crete. It is possible that they were simply too powerful; they had many ships and great wealth. However, the Minoans did have one great enemy—earthquakes. Sometime around 1700 BCE all the palaces and villas of Crete fell into ruins, only to be rebuilt soon after. This "second palace period" is the time of greatest Minoan influence and prosperity.

▶ The Minoan civilization grew up on the island of Crete and spread to other islands of the Aegean Sea and to mainland Greece.

MINOANS

c. 3000 BCE
Knossos and other large settlements are in place.

c. 1700 BCE
Palaces and villas of Crete collapse, probably after earthquakes. Beginning of "second palace period," the time of greatest Minoan prosperity.

c. 1625 BCE
Early date for explosion of volcano on Thera.

c. 1500 BCE
Traditional later date for Thera explosion.

c. 1450 BCE
Knossos and other Minoan palaces burn down; Mycenaean invasions begin.

▲ *The ruins of part of the Minoan palace of Phaistos in Crete, seventeenth century BCE.*

MINOAN RELIGION

Among the shrines for religious ceremonies at Knossos, one called the Shrine of the Double Axes has a double-ax design carved into its walls. In pillared rooms in palaces—at Hagia Triadha and Kato Zakro, for example—have been found clay vases and cups that contain the remains of food and tables where offerings were left for gods or goddesses.

The double-ax and bull-horn designs appear on many Minoan buildings and seem to have had a religious meaning. Small gold double axes have also been found deep in caves, sometimes embedded in stalactites, and at mountaintop shrines.

A Minoan Palace

In 1900 the British archaeologist Arthur Evans began excavations at Knossos that provided dramatic insights into Minoan Crete. A huge palace area was uncovered, with many rooms and a sewage and drainage system more advanced than that of the Romans. There were storerooms with jars of olive oil and wine and clay tablets with writing.

At the center was a great inner court, next to which a staircase led up and down to other stories. One group of rooms, probably a set of royal apartments, included a queen's sitting room, with leaping dolphins painted on its walls.

Minoan Art

Some palace rooms at Knossos are decorated with wall paintings, showing, for example, young men boxing and women in procession, dancing, or talking. One painting depicts a sport or religious ritual in which young men and women grasp the horns of an advancing bull and vault or somersault over its back.

Minoan civilization and art extended beyond Crete. For example, the town of Akrotiri on the island of Thera (present-day Santorini) has wall paintings similar in style to those at Knossos, including a striking one in which a young man carries a string of mackerel.

▼ *A rhyton (ceremonial drinking vessel) of gold and marble, in the shape of a bull's head, from Minoan Knossos, dating from between 1700 and 1400 BCE.*

The Burning of the Minoan Palaces

Around 1450 BCE many Minoan palaces were burned down, and the Minoan civilization came to an end. The new rulers of Crete were Mycenaeans, Greeks who had once traded with and now perhaps fought with the weakened Minoans. The Mycenaeans seem to have reoccupied Knossos but not the other palace sites.

If these events took place nearly two hundred years after Thera blew up, then Minoan civilization was not actually destroyed by the explosion itself, though it may have indirectly weakened the Minoans. They were perhaps made vulnerable by many deaths, both from the explosion and later from cancer-causing ash; by the loss of ships, harbors, and trade; and by the loss of animals and the lack of good food (the fields were choked for years afterward with pumice ash). Defensive walls from this late period found built around wells indicate the water supply was threatened by invaders.

Was Minoan Thera the Real Atlantis?

The fabled island of Atlantis haunted several Greek writers, including Plato. He wrote that he had been told of an island city of great wealth, surrounded by water, that was itself almost completely surrounded by land. This great city had vanished into the sea and was heard of no more.

Geologists say that when Thera blew up, it would have had the outline described in Plato's Atlantis tale, a basin with an island in the center, surrounded by water, itself surrounded by a high mountainous rim, or cordillera—the rim of the volcano. It is certainly possible that Atlantis was in fact a wealthy Minoan city on Thera.

THE EXPLOSION ON THERA

The volcanic explosion on Thera was perhaps the biggest in history. It buried the town of Akrotiri and probably ended life on the island. Did the huge tidal waves it generated, traveling the 70 miles (112 km) to Crete within hours, destroy Crete's harbors and kill thousands of people? Some writers have thought that the explosion's effect put an end to Minoan civilization.

However, Minoan (palace-centered) civilization on Crete seems to have continued until about 1450 BCE. When the explosion actually occurred is still debated. A date of 1500 BCE is often given, but it may have been much earlier, closer to 1625. Evidence for the 1625 date comes from long-lived Californian bristlecone pines and oak trees preserved in Irish peat bogs. Gaps in growth rings in some of these trees show loss of growth for years around that time, the implication being that the atmosphere was full of ash and smoke and that, as s result, less of the sun's warmth reached the earth.

◀ A view of the throne and wall paintings in the throne room of the palace of Knossos, dating from 1500 BCE.

Moche Culture

The Moche lived on the coast of northern Peru, between the ocean and the Andes mountain range. This civilization gets its name from the Moche River, which runs south of the modern-day Peruvian city of Trujillo and flows into the Pacific Ocean. The Moche peoples settled in the fertile land of this and other river valleys in the area but also learned how to channel water into drier areas. Most of what is known about the Moche comes from the remains of their buildings and from their impressive and beautiful pottery and metalwork. They flourished between 200 and 800 CE.

Everyday Life

Some Moche peoples fished, collected clams, and hunted seals. Most, though, farmed the land and occasionally hunted creatures such as deer. The Moche grew a wide variety of crops, including corn, peanuts, potatoes, beans, avocados, and chili peppers. They also kept guinea pigs, alpacas, llamas, and other animals. It seems that they were highly successful farmers, as they were able to grow enough to feed their growing population and still have time for art and leisure pursuits.

Only a few remnants of their cloth remain, but they indicate that the Moche were very artistic weavers. Also highly skilled metalworkers, the Moche smelted metals to produce bronze as well as copper and hammered sheets of copper, silver, and gold into three-dimensional shapes to form jewelry, masks, and headdresses. Metals were also occasionally used for more practical items, including spear tips, tweezers, and farm tools.

Watering the Land

The land surrounding the river valleys where the Moche lived was mainly desert. In order to farm successfully, the Moche became sophisticated irrigation engineers and achieved extraordinary technological feats. They built a large network of canals that channeled water from the rivers and fed it into the surrounding dry land. One canal brought water to farmland more than sixty miles (95 km) away. The irrigation

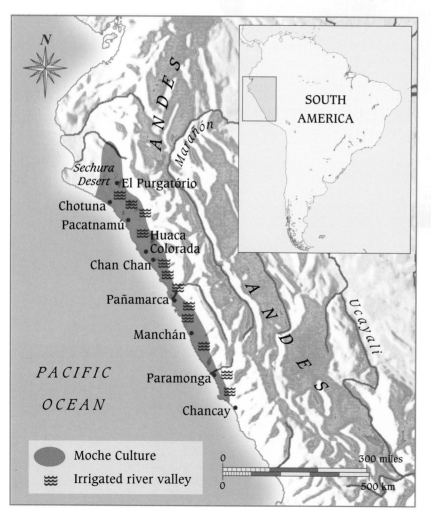

▼ The extent of the Moche culture's territory on the west coast of South America.

M O C H E   P O T T E R Y

The Moche had no written language but left behind a detailed record of their lives, work, and ceremonies in their pottery. They were highly skilled, and their work is considered to be some of the finest ancient art found in the whole of South America. They had two distinct styles of pottery, most of which was painted in reddish brown, white, and black. One type of pottery shows intricate painted scenes, often of unusual subjects, such as medical procedures, including amputation and the setting of broken arms and legs. The other type of pottery is decorated with molded three-dimensional figures, including humans, animals, and gods.

MOCHE CULTURE

c. 200 BCE

Moche culture begins.

200–700 CE

Moche civilization flourishes.

c. 200 CE

Lord of Sipan becomes a leader in Moche civilization.

800 CE

Moche civilization ends.

▼ Moche pottery often depicted human figures. This man with plaited hair is in fact a jar; the top of his head is removable.

network even included a simple but effective way of keeping the flow constant when water levels rose. Large square stones, known as brakes, were placed on the bottom of canals in certain places to reduce the water flow.

Moche Building

The canal systems were not the only structures that the Moche created. Their homes were built of adobe bricks molded from clay and left to dry in the sun. Trees that grew locally, such as the carob, provided the wood that the Moche used to make roof frames.

▲ *Huaca de la Luna (Temple of the Moon) consists of three platforms that rise just over 100 feet (32m) above the ground. Archaeologists believe that the site underwent at least six construction phases over more than five hundred years.*

The most impressive structures left behind by the Moche were a pair of massive temples in the shape of a pyramid, Huaca del Sol and Huaca de la Luna (Temple of the Sun and Temple of the Moon, respectively). The larger of the two, in fact the largest clay building found in the whole of South America, Huaca del Sol, is estimated to have been 1,100 feet (335 m) long, made from around 140 million clay bricks covered with a final layer of mud. Over half of it has been destroyed.

Class System and Sacrifice

Archaeologists believe that the Moche had a complicated class system. At the top of the class system were priests and warriors. Then came craftspeople and artisans, followed by fishermen and farmers, and finally servants, slaves, and beggars. The higher a person's class, the closer he or she lived to the temples found in the center of Moche settlements. Many scenes painted on Moche pottery depict the warriors and priests being honored—they are shown being carried by servants and wearing fine clothing. Other scenes show lower-class people being punished or even executed.

Sacrifice was also an important part of the Moche religion. Victims were put to death to keep the gods happy and to ensure that the rains came, the floods stayed away, and the crops kept growing. Scenes of ritual sacrifices to keep natural forces at bay have been found on excavated ceramics. Archaeologists have also discovered the skeletons of sacrificed people with their neck bones cut or broken, particularly around the site of Huaca de la Luna.

The Decline of the Moche

There are conflicting theories as to why the Moche civilization declined. Many of the scenes found on Moche pottery show

THE LORD OF SIPAN

Grave robbers and treasure hunters have stolen the contents of many Moche tombs and sites, so there was great excitement when an untouched Moche royal tomb was discovered in 1987 at the site of Sipan. The Moche ruler buried there was believed to have ruled around 200 CE and to have died at the age of forty. He has been called the Lord of Sipan. His skeleton was found in a casket made of cane and filled with solid gold jewelry and decorations. Alongside his casket were coffins containing three young women, a guard whose feet had been cut off, servants, a dog, and two llamas. It is believed that these people and creatures were sacrificed in order to assist the ruler in his journey to the afterlife. Hundreds of pots, filled at the time with food and water, were left in the tomb to sustain him on the journey.

◀ This royal tomb at the Moche site of Sipan has been reconstructed in its original location. Surrounding the central tomb are caskets containing the skeletons of some of the Moche ruler's subjects.

battles, and it is possible that other groups, possibly the Huari, invaded their territory and gained supremacy. However, scientific evidence points to a series of natural disasters, starting with a thirty-year drought around the end of the sixth century CE followed by floods and possibly earthquakes.

What is certain is that by 800 CE the Moche civilization had all but disappeared and had been replaced by the Huari culture.

SEE ALSO
• Chavín • Houses and Homes • Pottery

Mohenjo Daro

Mohenjo Daro is the modern name for an ancient city in the desert province of Sind, beside the Indus River, in present-day Pakistan. The site, buried under several mounds, was visited by archaeologists in the early 1900s. From the modern look of bricks found there, they assumed that the ruins were less than two hundred years old. In fact, Mohenjo Daro is almost five thousand years old and was one of the world's first true cities.

Mohenjo Daro was partly excavated in 1924 by the British archaeologist Sir John Marshall, who realized that he had discovered a previously unknown civilization. In the present day it is called the Indus valley or Harappan civilization, after Harappa, a similar city Marshall uncovered four hundred miles (640 km) to the northeast.

A Planned City

Mohenjo Daro was built around 2600 BCE, its streets neatly laid out on a grid plan. It has still not been fully excavated but is thought to have covered an area of about 617 acres (2.5 km²). Its population probably numbered between 35,000 and 50,000 people.

Like most Indus cities, Mohenjo Daro was divided into two areas. There was a high-walled citadel to the west, built on a raised platform of mud bricks. Buildings here included a huge granary and two assembly halls. Alongside the citadel was a bigger lower city, where most people lived and worked.

Water Management

The city's builders were highly skilled in water management. Houses were supplied with wells, bathing facilities, and toilets. Beneath the streets were deep brick drains, with manholes providing access so that they could be regularly cleaned.

The most unusual structure found in the city was a great sunken bath or pool, surrounded by a colonnade (row of columns). Skilfully constructed out of brick with steps leading down to a floor water-proofed with asphalt, it is thirty-six feet (12 m) long and nine feet (3 m) deep. It is not known how the bath was used, though it may have had a religious purpose. Bathing for religious reasons was a feature of later Indian society. Perhaps this ritual was a legacy of the Indus civilization.

▼ *The citadel of Mohenjo Daro. This ancient city, along with Harappa, was one of the two greatest urban centers of Harappan civilization.*

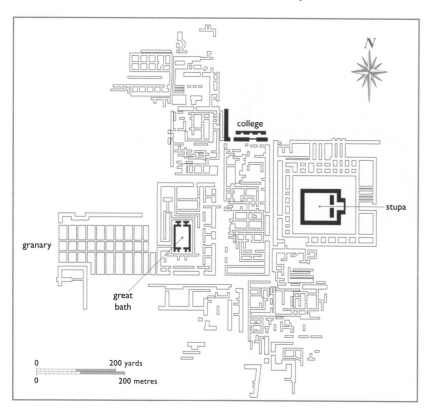

granary

college

stupa

great bath

0 — 200 yards
0 — 200 metres

N

Decline

Mohenjo Daro went into decline in the second millennium BCE, perhaps because the Indus River, on which the city depended, shifted its course. There is also evidence that the city was flooded on at least three occasions. By 1700 BCE Mohenjo Daro had been abandoned.

▲ Excavation at Mohenjo Daro reveals that the houses were built of sun-baked bricks made to a standard size—11 inches (28 cm) by 5.5 inches (14 cm) by 3 inches (7 cm).

IN 1924, ANNOUNCING THE DISCOVERY OF MOHENJO DARO, SIR JOHN MARSHALL WROTE THE FOLLOWING:

Hitherto India has almost universally been regarded as one of the younger countries of the world. . . . No monuments of note were known to exist of an earlier date than the third century BC. . . . Now, at a single bound, we have taken back our knowledge of Indian civilization some 3,000 years and have established the fact that in the third millennium before Christ, and even before that, the peoples of the Punjab and Sind were living in well-built cities and were in possession of a relatively mature culture with a high standard of art and craftsmanship and a developed system of pictographic [picture-based] writing.

CITED BY SIR JOHN CUMMINGS (ED.), REVEALING INDIA'S PAST, 1939

SEE ALSO
• Indus Valley

Money

Though a few civilizations have flourished without money, including for some time the Chinese and the Egyptian, coins and (later) paper money quickly became essential facilitators of trade and vital components of virtually every commercial culture in the ancient world.

Barter

In a money-free society goods were exchanged by means of a barter system. For example, two chickens might have been exchanged for a sack of wheat. Similarly, taxes were paid in the form of goods. In ancient Egypt, for instance, a high proportion of every farmer's crop—the tax—was placed in the pharaoh's storehouses.

This form of exchange and taxation worked quite well in societies that had little contact with outsiders and where the central authority of the king and his government was strong. Nevertheless, it had several drawbacks. First, trade involved much physical labor: goods had to be physically moved from place to place. Second, perishable goods, such as corn or fish, might rot and so lose their value before a suitable exchange material could be found. Third, barter was unwieldy: there could be no change from a deal, and it was not easy to keep accounts. Finally, it was difficult to pay wages in a purely barter society.

Rulers eventually found that replacing barter with money had definite political advantages. Taxes could be collected more easily and metal coins bearing the ruler's head were an excellent way of reminding people of his or her authority.

Forms of Money

The key effect of money was to separate the acts of selling and buying by adding a stage in between. Money stood for something other than itself: it represented the value of an object being exchanged. In other words, it was a substitute.

◀ *This Lydian coin from the sixth century* BCE *bears the royal emblem of a lion's head.*

The fact that money needed to be of value in itself led to various types of money. Sometimes oxen or sheep were used as currency. Several ancient peoples, such as the Celts, used cattle. In other societies, such as North America, India, and the Pacific islands, money took the form of shells, which were better suited to the purpose than cattle because they were smaller and more durable. So too were the pieces of stone and even teeth used by other cultures.

Metal Money

All these early forms of money were difficult to regulate and evaluate. The first metal money appeared in western Asia around 2000 BCE—there are early references to metal money in the Bible and the ancient Egyptians used *deben*, which were units of copper, silver, or gold. This early metal money was not in coin form but simply pieces of gold, silver, or alloy that were used as tokens in trade and exchange.

Some 1,300 years later the first coins appeared, in Lydia, Asia Minor. Made of a mix of gold and silver, they were oblong, with a mark stamped on them to indicate their purity and weight.

WAMPUM

The early native peoples of North America did not have money in the usual sense. Instead they used wampum, consisting of shell beads strung together in lines, which might then be woven into solid bands. Wampum was valuable because of the time and skill involved in its manufacture. It had several uses, including that of a ceremonial gift. When Europeans introduced the idea of money, wampum was naturally adapted to this purpose.

◀ This seventeenth-century beaded belt of wampum, crafted by a North American Iroquoian or Algonquian tribe, was made more as a gift than an article to be exchanged for goods or services.

▲ *This stamp, bearing an owl and olive branch (representing the city of Athens), was used for making tetradrachm coins of the fourth century BCE.*

coins and the amount of gold in the aureus ones.

At first, debasement made money for the government: it could make more coins from a given amount of precious metal. However, when the fraud was discovered, the value of the coins fell and thus prices rose, the resulting inflation seriously disrupting commercial activity.

The second money fraud involved stealing precious metal from the coins. Shaving the edge off a coin was known as "clipping." This practice was eventually stopped in modern times by giving coins a milled edge. Another fraud was shaking precious metal coins in a bag for a long period of time and collecting the valuable dust made as they clashed together, a practice called "sweating."

The March of Money

In about 330 BCE Alexander the Great created a royal mint at Babylon, which produced millions of hand-punched coins of standard weight and value. This innovation

By the sixth century BCE round coins with designs on each side, sometimes with a hole in the middle (as in China), had become widespread. Paper money was first used in China, around 700 CE.

Coins and Fraud

The advantages of metal coins over other forms of money were obvious. They could be easily graded, counted, stored, and transported. The value of an early coin depended on the weight of metal it contained.

However, metal coins were liable to two types of fraud. In the first, known as debasement, whoever issued the coinage (a king or his government) put a less-valuable metal into the coins than was marked on them. This activity was engaged in, for instance, by the Roman emperor Nero, who ruled from 54 to 68 CE. Nero reduced the amount of silver in the Roman denarius

AS SOON AS COINS APPEARED, PEOPLE BEGAN LENDING MONEY AND CHARGING INTEREST ON THE LOAN. THIS PRACTICE (USURY) WAS WIDELY CONDEMNED IN THE ANCIENT WORLD, NOT LEAST BY THE GREEK PHILOSOPHER ARISTOTLE:

Of all ways of getting wealth, the most hated, with good reason, is usury. . . . Money was meant to be used in exchange, not to grow with interest. In the latter case money is born out of money, the child being a copy of the parent. This is the least natural way to get rich.

ARISTOTLE, *POLITICS*

transformed the entire economy of Asia. Trade flourished as never before, and vast areas of the ancient world enjoyed the benefits it brought.

Despite the problems of debasement, clipping, and sweating, metal coinage had become a permanent feature of civilized society by the first century CE. Places that specialized in commerce, such as Athens and Phoenicia, could not have emerged without metal money.

Money also produced moral problems. Precisely because it brought earthly power and wealth, money was powerfully attractive. As a result, religious and moral teachers, especially among the early Christians, warned of the dangers that stemmed from a love of money for its own sake.

◀ *Known as the Alexander Hoard, this earthenware jug from the fourth century BCE was found to contain twenty one-drachma coins bearing the head of Alexander the Great.*

SEE ALSO

- Alexander the Great
- Aristotle • China
- Egypt • Nero
- Numbers • Trade

Monte Albán

Monte Albán was one of the first cities to be founded in the present-day Oaxaca region of southern Mexico, probably about 500 BCE.

The Rise and Fall of Monte Albán

Monte Albán was established by the Zapotec people, starting with a settlement of about five thousand people. A powerful ruling force of the Zapotecs controlled the Oaxaca valley from around 200 BCE, when the population reached about 15,000. From then until about 600 CE, the city had great power and influence as a trading center and ruling site.

Monte Albán was constantly in competition with the vast city-state of Teotihuacán to the northwest, and there was much trade and commerce between the two cities. From a peak of about 25,000 inhabitants in around 800 CE, Monte Albán declined and collapsed when local Zapotec leaders lost the people's support. The people moved and intermingled to find more fertile places to grow food and to find other trading partners. Teotihuacán also declined at this time.

What Was Monte Albán?

No one knows why such a big settlement as Monte Albán was established at this place. A hilltop at the head of three valleys was made level, and an acropolis built with

▼ *The main plaza at Monte Albán, the center of the Zapotec and Mixtec cultures.*

TEMPLE OF THE DANZANTES

Around Monte Albán's large main plaza are huge stone temples and palaces. The most famous of these is the Temple of the Danzantes (danzantes is the Spanish word for "dancers"). The carvings on the stones show over 140 male nude figures of all ages in various poses. Some of them look as if they are dancing or swimming. Their faces look angry or sad. In some of the pictures, designs have been carved on the men's groins, perhaps to mark ritual bloodletting. These carvings may depict the corpses of men killed in battles. The rulers of Monte Albán may have used this gruesome display as a warning or as a symbol of power.

▲ Some of the "danzante" stone carvings from the Temple of the Dancers. A speech glyph can be seen coming from the mouth of the nearest figure.

broad views of the landscape below. The hillsides were covered with terraces on which were built houses, storage pits, and shrines. Pyramids and palaces were built around a vast plaza, carefully laid out but with no space for cultivation and no obvious source of water. Although several miles of stone walls were also built, they did not form effective fortifications. They appear to have been simply a way of separating the city from the surrounding countryside. Was the city a symbol of power rather than a living, working community?

Features of Monte Albán

A ballcourt with an arena in which a two-team ball game was played has been uncovered in Monte Albán. Elaborate religious rituals probably took place in the plazas.

The Zapotecs, like the Maya people of later years, seem to have performed many religious rituals and ceremonies.

At one end of the main plaza, pointing toward the southwest, lies a mysterious arrow-shaped structure riddled with tunnels. Carvings in the walls outside depict scenes of death and destruction. Hieroglyphs that have not yet been decoded might be a record of battles won or places seized.

From one of the tunnels, it is possible to observe a star called Capella that appears only at the time of year when the sun is highest in the sky. Perhaps Monte Albán was a memorial to military victories or an early observatory to record the passing of the seasons. Some experts believe it may have been both.

SEE ALSO

• Maya

• Teotihuacán

• Zapotecs

Moses

According to the Bible, Moses was the Hebrew leader who led his people out of their slavery in Egypt and gave them God's laws, the Torah ("instruction"), which is the heart of Judaism. More than any other individual, Moses thus became the founder of the Jewish nation. Both Jews and Christians came to believe that he also wrote the first five books of the Bible, which were dictated to him by God.

The Biblical Story

The Bible says that Moses had a special relationship with God, who first spoke to him from a burning bush. God ordered him to lead the Hebrews out of Egypt, where they were enslaved. Moses, who stammered, did not want to take on this task and agreed only when God allowed him to use his brother Aaron as his spokesman.

When the pharaoh refused to let the Hebrews go, Moses called down ten terrible plagues on Egypt, each worse than the one before. The pharaoh finally relented when all the firstborn males in Egypt were killed.

▶ Moses with the tablets of the law. This wall painting dates from the sixth century CE and can be found in the Monastery of Saint Catherine on Mount Sinai in Egypt.

Moses then led his people to the "sea of reeds" (traditionally, the Red Sea), where he miraculously parted the waters so that the Hebrews could cross. He then closed the waters again, and the Egyptian army, which was pursuing them, drowned.

Ten Commandments

Moses climbed Mount Sinai, where God gave him ten laws, the Ten Commandments, inscribed on two stone tablets. The most important was the first commandment: "you shall have no other god before me." Moses was also given a mass of detailed laws covering moral behavior, religious worship, and every aspect of daily life. These laws form the core of the Torah and are still followed by practicing Jews.

Moses had a tabernacle (tent) made, a portable shrine that would be the focus of religious worship in the desert. At its center was a box, called the Ark of the Covenant, holding the stone tablets. The ark was later placed in the temple at Jerusalem. Moses also appointed his brother Aaron as the first high priest of the new religion.

To the Promised Land

Moses led the Hebrews for forty years in the Sinai Desert. He had to cope with challenges to his leadership, as well as backsliding by Hebrews who broke God's laws by worshiping a golden calf. God forgave the

Hebrews when they repented and finally let them enter what the Bible calls the "Promised Land" of Canaan.

Moses was allowed to see Canaan but not to enter it. He was said to have died at the age of 120 at the edge of the Promised Land.

Moses in History

The biblical story is the only record of the life of Moses. There is no mention of Moses or the Hebrews' escape from Egypt in any Egyptian source. There is no record of which pharaoh the story refers to or even when Moses lived. If Moses did exist, he must have lived before the 1220s BCE—the date of the earliest mention, in an Egyptian inscription, of Israel as a people in Canaan.

When the Bible story was finally written down in the Book of Exodus in the fifth century BCE, it drew on many traditions, and thus it is impossible to separate fact from legend. One example is the story that Moses was abandoned as a baby and then brought up by an Egyptian princess. Similar stories of abandonment are told of many legendary heroes, including the Greek Hercules and the Roman Romulus.

▲ In this fourteenth-century-CE wall painting of the Hebrews' flight from Egypt, the pursuing Egyptian soldiers drown as the waters of the Red Sea close over them.

THE COVENANT

When the Hebrews reached a mountain in the Sinai Desert, God spoke again to Moses, telling him that he had chosen the Hebrews as "a special treasure, above all other peoples" (Exodus 19:5). God made a covenant (pact or agreement) with the Hebrews: the Hebrews would receive God's protection and favors, including their own homeland, as long as they kept his laws.

Although historians cannot be certain about details of Moses' life and the miracles attributed to him, the truth may be that Moses was such an important historical figure that people told stories about him for generations, adding new details with each retelling. For instance, the story of the Exodus (that is, escape) from Egypt reached its final form during the sixth century BCE, when the Jews were again a captive people, in Babylon. The story affirmed the Jewish identity in a foreign land and would have explained why God had allowed the Jews to suffer such a disaster. The answer was that they had failed to keep God's laws. God's earlier forgiveness in the desert gave the Jews in Babylon hope that they would again be freed.

WHAT DOES MOSES' NAME MEAN?

Moses' name is Egyptian and means "son of," a word found in the names of many pharaohs, including Tuthmosis ("son of Thoth") and Ramses ("son of Ra"). Yet in the Bible the name is explained as a play on the Hebrew word mashah, meaning "drawn out of," because the infant Moses was drawn out of the bulrushes. It may be that the biblical account was written by a Jew who did not understand the Egyptian language.

◀ In European art Moses was sometimes shown with horns because of a line in the Vulgate, the fourth-century Latin translation of the Bible, that read, "Moses' head was horned." "Horned," however, is a misreading of the Hebrew word qaran, which actually means "shining."

SEE ALSO
- Babylon
- Hebrews
- Jerusalem
- Judaism

Mummification

Mummification is the preservation of a human or animal body in such a way that it retains a lifelike appearance. Strictly speaking, the word *mummification* refers only to the deliberate treatment of a corpse by people. However, the term is now also widely used to describe bodies that have been preserved by natural means.

Natural Desert Mummies

The oldest natural mummies are found in one of the earth's driest deserts, the Atacama, which lies along the Pacific coast of southern Peru and northern Chile. Around ten thousand years ago the people of the area buried their dead in the sand. The lack of rainfall and the dry air were perfect conditions for preserving a body by desiccation, that is, by drying it out.

A similar phenomenon occurred in China's Taklamakan Desert, where a cemetery was in use from about 1800 to 300 BCE. There, too, the bodies have completely dried out.

Natural Ice Mummies

Freezing can also lead to natural mummification. The preserved bodies of people of the Pazyryk culture of Siberia date to around 500 BCE. The region's permanently frozen ground has prevented the bodies of these people, their horses, and possessions from rotting away. The graves, dug into the permafrost, are of Pazyryk leaders, two of whom have been dubbed the Ice Warrior and the Ice Princess.

Natural Bog Mummies

In northern and western Europe peat bogs have also preserved human bodies by natural means. In these waterlogged places, where there is no oxygen to speed decay, where the temperature is low, and where the water contains tannic acid, flesh turns to leather.

Bog bodies date to Europe's Celtic period, between about 700 BCE and 200 CE. Some, such as Denmark's Tollund Man or England's Lindow Man, were sacrificial victims. They were killed and then thrown into the bogs as offerings to the gods.

◀ Tollund Man, who died around 100 BCE, had been strangled to death. His body was thrown into a Danish peat bog, which slowly turned his skin to leather and preserved him.

SIMILAUN MAN: THE ICEMAN

In 1991 in the Tyrolean Alps, Italy, a man's frozen body was found. His air-dried body, clothes, and possessions (including woven-grass clothes, a wooden-framed backpack, a copper-tipped ax, and bow and arrows) date him to about 3300 BCE. Popularly known as the Iceman, his is the oldest complete human body ever found. He died in his late forties, possibly after a fight in which he was badly injured. He fled 10,500 feet (3,200 m) up into the mountains and bled to death.

▶ Chinchorro mummies from Chile are the oldest known artificially mummified bodies. The first ones were made seven thousand years ago.

Mummies Made by People

Around 5000 BCE in the Atacama Desert region of Peru and Chile, people created mummies by stripping the skin from the dead and removing their internal organs. The bodies were left to dry, after which they were "rebuilt" with sticks, reeds, animal hair, clay, and paint. Mummies made this way by the Chinchorro people of Chile and Peru are some of the world's oldest intentionally mummified humans.

The best-known mummies are those made by the ancient Egyptians from around 2600 BCE to 400 CE. Egyptian embalmers removed all internal organs except the heart and kidneys. The body was washed and then filled and covered with natron, a mineral that dried it out. When dry, the body was rubbed with oils and resins to seal the skin and prevent rotting. Finally, it was wrapped in linen bandages, placed in a coffin, and buried.

SEE ALSO
- Celts
- Death and Burial
- Egypt

Music and Dance

The first music was probably the sound of drums made by cave people trying to communicate with each other across forests and plains. Neolithic hunters also played a primitive form of music, dancing to appease the spirits of the land and to ask for their help in the hunt. In 14,000 BCE the people of what is now Ukraine were using mammoth tusks as percussion instruments.

As people began to settle on farms and grow crops, around 10,000 BCE, music took on another role. It helped farm laborers to work in rhythm. Songs kept their minds off the monotony of sowing and harvesting. In the temples and at open-air altars, music accompanied the dancing in fertility rites.

Drums and Other Instruments

Drums featured a great deal in primitive music. In around 6,000 BCE people in Moravia were stretching animal skin over sections of hollowed-out tree trunk. They beat the drums with their hands, using their palms to get deep, vibrating sounds. Later, in the Fertile Crescent (the land in western Asia between the Tigris and the Euphrates Rivers) and the countries around the Mediterranean, drums were made of pottery or iron. By 4000 BCE the Egyptians were tying the skins on to their drums with thongs. A thousand years later the Mesopotamians had frame drums, which could be round, square, or octagonal in shape. Some had small metal bells attached. By 2800 BCE the people of Ur were also playing an early form of harp, and by 2300 BCE the Babylonians had developed the flute.

▶ Reconstruction of a bull-headed lyre, from Ur in Mesopotamia, dated around 2500 BCE. This instrument, similar to a harp, is made of wood, shell, and bitumen and decorated with gold and lapis lazuli.

▲ *In this third-century-BCE Greek terra-cotta, the girl on the left is playing a kithara, and the girl on the right is playing a lute.*

Egyptian Music and Dance

Egyptian drums were played by men and women, both of whom played a range of instruments. Harps were very popular in Egypt, as well as in Mesopotamia, Persia, Africa, and India. Music was a vital part of Egyptian life. The instruments Egyptians played included harps, flutes, lyres, trumpets, drums, cymbals, tambourines, and a sacred rattle called a sistrum.

Dancing was also very much part of Egyptian culture. It took place in festivals, in the marketplace, during banquets, in harems, and in temples, to please the gods. Even the king sometimes danced. For example, at Dendera, at the cult center of Hathor, patron of music and dancing, one

of the hymns describes the king dancing for the goddess with "his sistrum of gold."

Dancers were frequently hired to entertain at parties, while the rich kept servants to perform at banquets. Women dancers often wore a jeweled belt around their waist. Egyptian performers used clappers (much like Spanish castanets), as well as tambourines.

Greek Music and Dance

The ancient Greeks, whose culture flourished from around 1000 BCE, believed that music had a powerful effect on the soul and on people's actions. People played music in the home, on the streets during festivals, at funerals, and in the temple when they offered sacrifices. Music was used during theatrical performances to set the mood and to heighten the dramatic effect of key scenes. It was also played as an accompaniment to dance and poetry. Music was so important to the Greeks that their education was largely based on teaching music (a subject that included drama and literature) and sport.

The two main religious cults in ancient Greece were dedicated to the gods Apollo and Dionysus. The followers of Apollo, the god of the sun and reason, preferred the music of the kithara, which looked very much like a handheld harp and was said to instill clarity and simplicity of thought in its listeners. The followers of Dionysus, the god of passion, ecstasy, and wine, preferred the more enchanting music of the aulos, a reed instrument that was thought to fill its listeners with passion.

Dance was also an important part of Greek life. There were more than two hundred different dances, including ones for religious festivals, harvests, weddings, and athletic performances. The Greeks even had special dances for funerals, as did the ancient Egyptians.

HORN MUSIC

The horn is one of the most ancient musical instruments in the world. Stone Age people used animal horns to call one another across vast forests. During the Bronze Age the people of Denmark made metal horns called lurs, shaped like mammoth tusks. The horn was played in Mesopotamia, Egypt, Greece, and South and West Africa. A ram's horn, called a shofar, was used by the ancient Hebrews as a warning call or to gather the various tribes. The shofar is still sounded in synagogues during the festival of Rosh Hashanah.

▼ This wind instrument from ancient China, with an elaborately detailed mouthpiece and bell, was sculpted from a hollowed-out human thigh bone.

Chinese Music

The ancient Chinese regarded music as a sacred art. By the ninth century BCE Chinese musicians were playing a form of the modern transverse flute, which the player blows on sideways. By the time of the Shang dynasty, which began in 1600 BCE, the Chinese had a variety of instruments, including chimes, drums, bells, and other wind and string instruments.

▶ This fresco from Cicero's villa in the ruined city of Pompeii shows street musicians in ancient Rome around 100 BCE.

Roman Music and Dance

The ancient Romans inherited the Greeks' love of music in private and public places. Military and triumphal parades in Rome were accompanied by the sound of drums and fanfares of trumpetlike horns, as they had been in ancient Egypt.

The Romans adapted Greek mythology into pantomime. It was performed by a chorus of singers, an orchestra, and dancers. The chief dancer narrated the story, using stylized gestures and movements. There were two kinds of dancers in ancient Rome—amateurs, who were taught simple dance steps, and professionals, who performed pantomime gestures, using their body, hands, and facial expressions to denote character and emotion.

Musical entertainments were also staged in the homes of the rich to delight guests at dinner. In addition, people could attend musical concerts, which usually featured harps and singers.

Music with loud drums and cymbals was played in the arena as the gladiators entered and exited at the end of the gladiatorial games and while people were being initiated into secret societies dedicated to the gods. A gentler music was played in temples. It survived the arrival of Christianity and was the forerunner of sacred music and hymns.

IN 50 BCE THE POET LUCRETIUS DESCRIBED A PROCESSION IN HONOR OF CYBELE, A GREEK GODDESS ALSO WORSHIPED IN ROME:

The Galli come:
And hollow cymbals, tight-skinned tambourines
Resound around to bangings of their hands;
The fierce horns threaten with a raucous bray;
The tubed pipe excites their maddened minds.

LUCRETIUS, ON THE NATURE OF THINGS

SEE ALSO

• Art • Drama • Festivals • Masks
• Sports and Entertainment • Religion

Mycenaean Civilization

For more than four hundred years, between about 1650 and 1200 BCE, Mycenae, in the northeast of the Peloponnese, was the leading city of Greece. The discovery of its treasures in the late nineteenth century was an archaeological event of tremendous historical importance.

A Grave at Mycenae

In 1876 German archaeologist Heinrich Schliemann discovered a remarkable hoard of treasure in a circular grave at Mycenae. The dead had been buried with objects made of gold, silver, bronze, and alabaster. Ornate swords and daggers lay around the bodies, along with drinking vessels, some made from ostrich eggs. The women wore jewelry, the men wore gold masks, and the children were wrapped in gold leaf.

Schliemann had been looking for historical evidence of the world of Homer's warring heroes, as described in the *Iliad* between around 750 and 700 BCE. He thought he had found it. Homer's "past," though, was not one historical period. In the *Iliad* the poet assembled stories, ideas, and objects from several eras, including that of the Mycenaeans.

Schliemann's discoveries were dated to between about 1600 and 1550 BCE. They reveal several things about the early Mycenaeans. Their rulers—some of whom were nearly six feet (1.8 m) tall—were wealthy. They had many weapons, employed highly skilled craftsmen, and were great traders.

Mycenaean Trade

The Mycenaeans' trade developed as their influence spread. They traded with Minoan Crete and other Aegean islands and with Europe and Egypt for amber, ostrich eggs, and ivory. They sent pottery containing perfumed oil east to Cyprus, southeast to Egypt, and west to Malta and Sardinia. Mycenaean olive oil, wine, pottery, and objects of gold and bronze went far afield, including to western Asia.

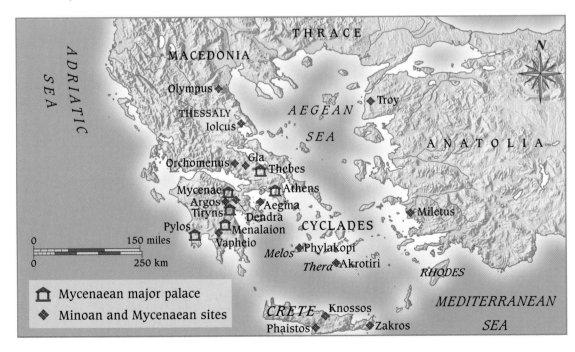

◀ *Mycenaean Greece (c. 1550–1150 BCE), including the major palaces and Mycenaean and Minoan sites.*

The Palace Period of Mycenaean Civilization

After about 1500 BCE the Myceneans, like the Minoans before them, built palaces, at Mycenae itself, at Tiryns, and at Pylos. There are also signs that palaces were built during this period at Thebes and Athens.

The amount of weaponry found in graves might suggest that Mycenaean Greece was riddled by internal conflict. Yet Mycenae was the center of a network of roads and bridges connecting with other towns, such as Pylos. This construction, which must have required cooperation, would have been really useful only in peace. The defensive walls were built late in Mycenaean times, in the fourteenth and thirteenth centuries BCE, perhaps in response to some outside threat.

Prosperity and Pylos

At Pylos, in the southwest of the Peloponnese, is the best-preserved palace of Mycenaean times. The palace had a throne room, with a great hearth in the center, and above it a decorated balcony. Many walls—and even the floor of the throne-room—were decorated with paintings depicting battles, hunts, musicians, and processions.

There were storerooms for wine, olive oil, grain, and arms. In one room were 2,853 drinking glasses; in another, more than five thousand cups, bowls, and drinking vessels. Clay tablets, used for state

▼ *A view of the Lion Gateway at the entrance to the palace of Mycenae, part of the defensive fortifications built in the fourteenth and thirteenth centuries BCE.*

3500   3000   2500   2000   1500   1000   500   1   500

MYCENAEAN CIVILIZATION

1600–1200 BCE

Mycenae is leading city of Greece.

c. 1500 BCE

Beginning of Mycenaean palace period.

c. 1450 BCE

Mycenaeans begin to take control of most of Crete; they occupy Knossos after its destruction.

c. 1380 BCE

Control of Knossos ends with another mysterious destructive event.

c. 1200 BCE

Mycenaean civilization collapses.

records, were baked hard in the fire that wrecked the palace sometime around 1200 BCE. One tablet shows the names of two oxen, Glossy and Blackie. On others are names of gods that have been identified as Zeus, Hera, and Athena—the gods of the later Greeks.

The End of the Mycenaean World

Some time after 1450 BCE, the Mycenaeans took control of most of Crete and occupied Knossos after its destruction. They probably controlled Knossos until another mysterious catastrophe in about 1380 BCE.

▲ A reconstruction of the thirteenth-century-BCE Mycenean palace at Pylos, in the Greek Peloponnese. The palace was destoyed by fire around 1200 BCE.

HEINRICH SCHLIEMANN DESCRIBES HIS EXTRAORDINARY FIND AT MYCENAE IN 1876:

I have just discovered what I take to be the skeleton of a woman, judging from the small teeth and the female ornaments with which the bones were covered. The two earrings are treasures in themselves. There were pendants of precious stones [red], hundreds of large and small leaves of gold, every one entirely covered with spiral ornaments and circles. When, after having dug out mountains of earth, I began to remove the stones and rubbish of the lower layer, I struck on a large gilded silver cow's head with two golden horns and one large cup of gold with a pigeon on each handle. . . . The bones I found are like the bones of giants. . . . Close to them were large heaps of lances and swords of bronze. . . . This tomb is that which the traditions of the ancient Greeks assigned to the "king of men," "wide-ruling Agamemnon."

HEINRICH SCHLIEMANN, MYCENAE

Around 1200 BCE the Mycenaean civilization seems to have collapsed. Mycenae itself was burned down. From Lefkandi and Iolkos, north of Athens, to Khania on Crete, settlements were burned and abandoned.

Historians offer a number of explanations, including an invasion of Dorians from the north or a local rising against palace rulers. One interesting theory is that, after the collapse of the Hittite Empire in Anatolia, the Aegean Sea became infested with pirates. Trade would have become dangerous and the Mycenaeans could no longer have imported gold and silver or grain.

Despite this collapse, some sites—such as Tiryns and Mycenae—were rebuilt. Life continued, even on Crete, in settlements inhabited by fewer people, with a much simpler way of life. At Pylos people moved down to the coast. Palace accounts were no longer kept, and so the skill of writing was lost, and a "dark age" began.

▼ A fragment of a clay tablet from Knossos in Mycenean times, around 1450 BCE. The tablet, baked hard by fire, records in Linear B some details of palace life.

LINEAR A AND B

Linear A is the name of the script that the Minoans, who spoke a non-Greek language, used for written records. It has not yet been deciphered. The Mycenaeans adopted the Minoans' script to keep records of agriculture, land ownership, industrial production, the storage of wine and olive oil, and so on. About a thousand inscribed tablets were found at Pylos and Knossos. Others come from Tiryns, Thebes, and Mycenae.

The Mycenaean version of the script was deciphered in 1952 by two English scholars, Michael Ventris and John Chadwick. They showed that the Mycenaeans spoke an early kind of Greek and gave the Mycenaean script the name Linear B.

SEE ALSO
- Acropolis • Archaeology • Architecture
- Art • Athens • Cycladic Culture
- Iliad and Odyssey • Knossos • Minoans
- Trade • Troy • Writing

Mythology

Myths are stories that are based on popular beliefs or that explain natural or historical events. In ancient times myths developed as they were passed on, changing with the societies in which they were told. Many myths describe gods and their relationships with each other and with humans. The gods may represent certain aspects of life, such as love, death, and war. Myths also tell of heroes who set an example to their people or who win them something they need, such as fire. These heroes often save their people from destruction by fighting monsters or even the gods themselves.

Myths and Legends

Some myths may have originated as the visions of individual shamans or tribal priests and priestesses. These myths were passed on to the tribe and probably used in magical rituals, for example, to heal the sick or to encourage crops to grow. In some cultures they are still used in this way.

Other myths began as legends. Legends may start as stories of real people and events, but the stories get exaggerated and added to as centuries pass. Elements of the ordinary tend to disappear from legends over time. The hero of many a legend-based myth retains no unheroic qualities at all.

Hero Myths

Hero myths are about great men—and sometimes women—who inspire their people. Typical heroes come from a poor or mysterious background. Often they have to go and seek a father figure, proving their courage on the way. They may be sent on a dangerous quest, in which they are helped by a god or goddess.

▶ This first-century-BCE wall painting from Pompeii depicts the gods Mars and Venus relaxing. Mars's battle helmet and shield lie idle. The winged figure of Cupid looks on at the two lovers.

► Found in the tomb of Tutankhamen, this golden pectoral (part of a necklace) shows Tutankhamen as Osiris, god of the underworld, protected by the twin goddesses of Egypt, Wadjyt the snake and Nekhbet the vulture. It dates from around 1330 BCE.

Cuchulainn, from Irish mythology, is a good example of a hero. According to stories dating from the first century BCE, he was born mysteriously in a poor cottage, perhaps the son of a god who had visited the boy's mother in a dream. He set off in search of adventure and found a "father," King Conchobor of Ulster.

In one special type of hero myth, the hero brings back knowledge or something of great importance to the tribe, such as sacred rituals or weapons. In another type, the hero is a god who dies after sacrificing himself for his people and is somehow reborn. Examples include the Welsh Lleu Llaw Gyffes (from the *Mabinogion*), the Egyptian Osiris, and the Norse Odin.

Creation Myths

The earliest myths explain the creation of the universe. For example, according to some ancient Greek, Chinese, and Egyptian myths, the universe hatched from an egg. In other creation myths, such as those of Native Americans, the first people on earth emerge from a cave or out of a great flood.

Explanatory Myths

Some myths explain natural phenomena, such as features of the landscape, the existence of men and women, or why humans cannot understand animals. One Native American myth explains why a certain tall rock had deep grooves on it. The marks were said to have been made by the claws of a giant bear trying to reach some hunters who had climbed up the rock to escape.

Lands-of-the-Dead Myths

Finally there are myths in which the hero visits the land of the dead. This world can be grim, as when Odysseus descends into Hades or the Sumerian goddess Inanna goes to visit her sister Ereshkigal, queen of the underworld. In other cases, though, it can be a land of light, laughter, and feasting. These surroundings are what the Celtic hero Oisin finds when he rides away with a fairy woman. However, when the hero wants to return home he usually finds that hundreds of years have passed in the ordinary world. When Oisin's feet touch Irish soil once more, he immediately ages three hundred years.

MYTHS AROUND THE WORLD

There are remarkable similarities between myths worldwide. Some scholars say this coincidence shows that human beings everywhere are similar, and thus they develop the same stories. Others think that traveling traders passed the myths on from one community to another.

One common theme is that of earth goddesses and sky gods destroying their children. For example, the Polynesian sky god Rangi and his wife Papa accidentally crushed their children, and the Greek sky god Ouranos stuffed his children back inside the earth mother Gaia.

Underworld descents are another well-known subject. For instance, the Greek hero Orpheus went down into Hades to ask for his dead wife. He won her back but was told not to look at her until they reached the surface. He could not resist and lost her forever. Several Native American myths are very similar, including one from the Zuni tribe. Other mythical deities who went on missions into the land of the dead include the Sumerian goddess Inanna and, in Norse myth, Odin's son Hermod, who went to rescue his brother Balder.

Similar myths about the creation of gods often describe one pantheon of gods fighting and replacing an older one. The Greek Olympians and the Babylonian gods, headed by the warrior god Marduk, are both examples of such a new generation of gods.

▼ A sixth-century-BCE amphora depicting Orpheus playing his lyre to the goddess Athena. Orpheus's playing was so beautiful that it calmed storms and persuaded Hades to give Orpheus back his dead wife.

HOW CUCHULAINN GOT HIS NAME

As a young child, Cuchulainn was named Setanta. At the age of six, he amazed King Conchobor by his strength and skill at games. He beat all the other boys at hurling (a game similar to hockey) single-handed. So Conchobor invited the boy to join him at a feast being held by Culann the Smith. Setanta agreed to follow later.

Conchobor and his warriors arrived and were greeted by Culann.

"Is that all of you?" asked the smith. "I have a fierce guard dog, and if you're all here I'll set him loose outside."

Forgetting his invitation to the boy hero, Conchobor agreed.

Meanwhile Setanta set off. He played as he went, tossing up his ball, aiming a stick at it, and then hurling a spear after them both and catching it before it hit the ground. When he approached Culann's house, the huge hound charged snarling toward him.

Setanta calmly watched the dog and then hurled his ball so hard into the animal's open jaws that it shot down its throat and disemboweled it. Hearing the noise, Conchobor's men rushed outside and were relieved to find the boy alive and well. Culann, however, was downcast—he had lost his dog.

The boy reassured the man: "Don't worry. I'll rear a pup and train him. Until that pup is ready, I'll be your guard dog myself!"

Thus, Setanta earned the name Cuchulainn—the Hound of Culann.

The death of Cuchulainn. Wounded, Cuchulainn strapped himself to a stone so that he could die standing up. He was killed by Erc and Lughaid (both shown). The three women (bottom left) are the daughters of Calatin, witches who helped to cause Cuchulainn's death.

Nebuchadrezzar II

Born in 630 BCE, Nebuchadrezzar II was the last great Babylonian king. The Babylonian form of his name, Nabu-kudurri-usur, means "Oh Nabu, watch over the heir." (Nabu was the son of Marduk, the main Babylonian god.) Nebuchadrezzar enlarged his empire at the expense of his neighbors, but he is also thought to have built the Hanging Gardens of Babylon, one of the wonders of the ancient world.

A Soldier King

Nebuchadrezzar was the eldest son of Nabopolassar. A strong ruler, Nabopolassar was constantly at war with the neighboring Assyrians. By the time Nebuchadrezzar was twenty, he had joined his father's army as an administrator. In about 606 BCE he accompanied Nabopolassar on a military expedition in the mountains north of Assyria. He proved himself a good army leader, and in 605 BCE Nabopolassar sent him on a mission to Syria to regain Babylonian territory lost to the Egyptians. Again Nebuchadrezzar triumphed, routing the Egyptian army at the city of Carchemish. This victory put the whole of Syria under Babylonian control. On August 16 of that year Nabopolassar died. Nebuchadrezzar returned to Babylon, and three weeks later he was crowned king.

The Sacking of Jerusalem

No sooner had the new king been crowned than he sought to extend his empire even farther. One state after another fell before his armies, including the Hebrew kingdom of Judah. Judah became part of the Babylonian Empire, and the Hebrews were forced to swear loyalty to Nebuchadrezzar.

When the Jewish people revolted against his rule, Nebuchadrezzar retaliated. On March 15, 597 BCE, he attacked the city of Jerusalem. About ten thousand Jews were exiled to Babylon, including Jehoiachin, the king of Judah, and many of his nobles. Nebuchadrezzar placed Jehoiachin's uncle, Zedekiah, on the throne of Judah as a puppet king.

This engraving, based on a story from the Old Testament Book of Daniel, shows Nebuchadrezzar speaking to his court with his followers at his feet.

NEBUCHADREZZAR'S BUILDINGS

Nebuchadrezzar finished the fortification of Babylon that his father had started, adding a moat and an outer wall to keep the enemy out. A devout man, he rebuilt the city's temples and paved with limestone the Holy Way, along which the statue of Marduk (the chief Babylonian god) was carried. He is also said to have built the famous Hanging Gardens, thought to be a present for his wife, Queen Amyitis, who missed the greenery and cool breezes of her childhood home in the mountainous country of Media.

Zedekiah rebelled against Babylon in 588 and 587 BCE, and Nebuchadrezzar besieged Jerusalem once again. In 586 BCE he destroyed it completely. Jerusalem's temple was burned to the ground, and Nebuchadrezzar took what was left of the Jewish population into captivity.

Yet, compared with other kings of his time, Nebuchadrezzar was very considerate toward exiles living in Babylon. Many Jewish captives from Jerusalem were promoted to quite important positions at the Babylonian court. The Jewish prophets Jeremiah and Ezekiel both praised the king in their writings.

Death of the King

Nebuchadrezzar died in 561 BCE and was succeeded by Nabonidus, a nobleman who was often absent from Babylon. The Babylonian Empire was left open to attack, and in 539 BCE the city of Babylon was sacked by the Persian king Cyrus the Great. Some three hundred years later the Macedonian general Seleucus became the ruler of Babylon. He deserted it to build a new capital city on the banks of the Tigris River, and Nebuchadrezzar's temples and buildings were left to fall into ruins.

◀ An engraving showing the Babylonians slaughtering King Zedekiah's children after the Jewish uprising of 588 and 587 BCE. The massacre was part of the terrible punishment inflicted on the Israelites for their opposition to Babylonian rule.

SEE ALSO

- Architecture • Assyrians • Babylon
- Babylonians • Belshazzar • Cyrus the Great
- Hebrews • Jerusalem • Macedonians
- Marduk

Nefertiti

Nefertiti, perhaps the daughter of an important noble, was the chief wife of Akhenaten, who ruled Egypt from 1352 to 1336 BCE. They had six daughters but no sons. Akhenaten did have at least one son, Tutankhamen, by a minor wife named Kiya, but Akhenaten is only ever shown with the family he had with Nefertiti. One of their daughters, Ankhesenpaaten, married her half brother Tutankhamen, who later became pharaoh.

Nefertiti was not only a favorite wife but also a close adviser to Akhenaten. Statues and carved and painted scenes show Nefertiti taking part in religious ceremonies with Akhenaten, sometimes as an assistant, sometimes as an equal or even as the main figure. She is occasionally shown wearing an unusual blue crown that no queen before or after her seems to have worn, another sign that she was special to the pharaoh. Finally, Nefertiti is also shown fighting the enemies of the pharaoh. Usually only the pharaoh was shown fighting enemies. If, as many Egyptologists believe, Nefertiti succeeded her husband as king, she was one of six female pharaohs of ancient Egypt.

Life in Amarna

Living in their new capital city, Amarna, in an isolated location, the royal family chose to remove themselves from events traditionally at the center of life in Egypt. They made many changes, especially to the religion, but seem not to have foreseen how unpopular these changes would be.

They certainly did little to stop neighboring countries from breaking free of Egyptian control and even taking land from Egypt. Ancient letters found among the ruins of Amarna include increasingly desperate ones from generals and governors of border provinces begging for replies to their letters about these problems.

◀ *This bust of Nefertiti was found in the city of Amarna, in the workshop of the sculptor Tuthmosis. She is wearing her special crown.*

THE ROYAL FAMILY

Family life was of great importance to the ancient Egyptians. Tombs of Egyptian families were often carved with images of a husband and wife side by side or holding hands. Pharaohs, however, were not usually depicted in this way on their tombs, because they were believed to be more than just ordinary people: they were a link between people and gods and so were partially godlike themselves. Nefertiti and Akhenaten broke with this tradition. At Amarna, their new capital city, they influenced the development of a naturalistic style in Egyptian art. They encouraged artists to show the royal family as a normal family. Thus, the royal couple appeared in paintings and carvings in a family setting, playing with their daughters.

▶ Detail of a carving of Nefertiti kissing one of her daughters. Akhenaten and Nefertiti were the only royal couple who had carvings and paintings made of themselves playing with their children.

Nefertiti's Last Years

After about 1340 BCE, there is no further mention of Nefertiti in Egyptian records, so 1340 may be the year of her death. The tomb of Nefertiti has not yet been found. Someone named Smenkhkara ruled Egypt for two years after Akhenaten and before Tutankhamen. Some historians believe Nefertiti changed her name to Smenkhkara and ruled Egypt alone, perhaps as a female pharoah. Other historians believe that Smenkhkara may have been an older brother of Tutankhamen.

Buried Truths

Exactly what happened to Nefertiti is not clear, because the mummies of Akhenaten and Nefertiti have not been identified. Some historians think they have identified Smenkhkara's tomb, but even this claim is uncertain. There was chaos in Egypt around the time of Akhenaten's death. Later rulers, Horemheb and Ramses II, deliberately portrayed Akhenaten's rule as a temporary setback in the smooth course of Egypt's history. Amarna was deserted and the capital moved back to Thebes.

Nero

Nero (37–68 CE), who ruled the Roman Empire from 54 to 68 CE, was born Lucius Domitius Ahenobarbus. Nero, his family's nickname for him, means "brave" or "energetic." Nero was very interested in the arts. He drew, painted, composed poetry, and sang songs, pursuits that made him very popular with artists and actors but unpopular with the aristocrats, who disapproved of the emperor associating with common entertainers.

The Troubled Succession

Nero succeeded the emperor Claudius, who is thought to have been poisoned by Nero's mother, Agrippina. For the first few years of his reign, the new emperor was largely guided by his mother, by his tutor, Seneca, and by Burrus, a commander of the Praetorian Guard. The result was a period of peace and stability. However, Nero was afraid that Claudius's son Britannicus would try to become emperor and so had him poisoned in 55 CE. Later Nero came to believe that Agrippina was also a threat. Despite the fact that she was his mother, he had her murdered in 59, after which his reputation appears to have grown steadily worse. He dismissed Seneca and quarreled with the Roman senate. Taxes were raised, and wealthy men had their land confiscated.

Fire and Conspiracy

In 64 the Great Fire of Rome destroyed more than half the city. Some people accused Nero of starting it himself in order to make room to build his magnificent palace, known as the Golden House. This rumor was probably spread by his enemies, although it is certainly true that Nero did have his palace built on the ashes. To deflect blame from himself, Nero accused the Christians of starting the blaze.

In 65 and 66 two conspiracies to murder Nero were uncovered. Those involved were put to death or exiled. Because some of the conspirators were senators, Nero declared that he hated the entire senate.

◀ A portrait bust of Nero dating from around 75 CE.

In 68 CE some of the legions posted in the Roman provinces tried to declare one of their own leaders emperor, as they no longer had faith in Nero. Support grew for Servius Sulpicius Galba, a Roman governor, and so Nero decided to leave Rome. After he had left the city, the prefect Nymphidius Sabinus declared that the Praetorian Guard would follow Galba. Nero was finally tracked down to his villa just outside Rome, where, before committing suicide, he declared, "What an artist dies in me!" He was only thirty years old.

Legacy

Nero's persecution of the Christians and the murder of his mother have given him a reputation for being an evil tyrant. However, although he was certainly ruthless in punishing those who opposed him, Nero was popular with the common people and known for his acts of generosity. Had it not been for the events of the Great Fire and Nero's failure to understand that a successful emperor needs the support of the army, his reign might have turned out very differently.

▶ An example of the ornate wall paintings in Nero's Golden House. The chief painter, Famulus (or Fabulus), framed popular scenes from Roman mythology and romantic landscapes with floral motifs.

SEE ALSO

- Agrippina
- Claudius
- Roman Republic and Empire
- Rome, City of
- Tacitus

Glossary

adobe A brick made from sun-dried earth and straw.

ahau A Mayan lord, part king, part high priest, who ruled over a city region.

asphalt An oily black substance that seeps out of the ground. When melted over a fire, mixed with sand, and then poured onto the ground, it forms a hard waterproof surface.

atoll A ring-shaped island made of coral, partly or completely enclosing an area of seawater.

bloodletting Ritual cutting of the body to take blood; done to mark a birth, death, or marriage or as a cleansing rite.

cistern A tank or vessel used for storing water.

desiccation The process of drying something out.

dowry The money or property brought by a woman to her marriage.

gild Cover with gold leaf.

glyph A small picture, image, or sign representing a sound or idea, as in Mayan writing.

gold leaf Gold hammered out until it is paper-thin.

granary A building for storing grain.

harem A place where rulers in the ancient world kept their many wives.

lapis lazuli A bright blue mineral used as a gemstone.

macana A sword with a wooden handle and a sharp blade made from obsidian or flint.

matrilineal Referring to the passing on of names and property through the mother rather than the father.

milpa An open space in a forest cleared by burning vegetation, the ash from which fertilizes the ground.

natron A white, yellow, or gray mineral once used in embalming and as a soap.

pantheon All the gods of a given culture or people.

peat Partially rotted organic matter preserved in a waterlogged oxygen-free environment.

permafrost Permanently frozen layer of ground in low-temperature regions of the earth.

Praetorian Guard The Roman emperor's personal bodyguard, numbering several thousand soldiers with two commanders.

procurator A Roman official who governed a province. The procurator oversaw tax collection and maintained law and order.

pumice A light, porous rock formed from solidified lava.

scimitar A curved sword.

sexagesimal Based on the number sixty.

shaman Someone believed to be able to enter the spirit world on behalf of his or her people.

stalactite An icicle-like hanging rock formation composed of water mixed with half-dissolved limestone.

stela A tall stone monument with an altar at the base, often carved with glyphs portraying animal gods or describing the lives and victories of great kings.

stylus A pointed instrument, usually a reed, used in ancient times for writing on clay.

tablet An object, usually of clay or wood, made to receive an inscription.

tannic acid A colorless liquid obtained from tree bark used to convert animal skins into leather.

taro A starchy root crop cooked as a vegetable and also ground to make a sort of bread.

usury The lending of money for a fee, often a large one.

wampum In North America, woven beads used by various native peoples as money or as a ceremonial gift.

Index

Page numbers in **boldface type** refer to main articles.
Page numbers in *italic type* refer to illustrations.